Paint by Numbers

The Art of Fatherhood

By

Brian B. LaFauci

Edited By

Richard Plate & Joan LaFauci

I would like to thank the following people:

My Parents, for providing me the framework to grow into my own parent and the love to do it differently without judgement.

My Wife, for supporting all my endeavors and for her commitment to merging our Brady Bunch family into what it is today. Much of what I write about has evolved from watching us parent together.

My Children, for the joy and happiness they bring into our lives, but mostly, for the inspiration behind this book.

My Sister, for being the clear headed sounding board I often need and the daily motivation to go beast mode.

My Brother-In-Law and Paul Juneau, for turning my words into a beautiful song with the obvious help of a masterful producer!

Download the Paint by Numbers Song.

I cannot think of any need in childhood as strong as the need for a father's protection.

— Sigmund Freud

Paint By Numbers

Introduction

An Ordinary Artist

Paint By Numbers

It is with the most pronounced surety, that from this pulpit I shall proclaim the works of Rembrant, Donatello and Bach, as well as those of Swift, Doig and Penone, as diminutive in juxtaposition to the life-long tapestry actualized through the acts of an ordinary father upon a child.

Make no mistake about it, fatherhood, and parenting in the more global sense, is an art. It depicts every aspect that makes art beautiful, alluring, thought provoking and worthy of discussion. Its interpretation can easily transform when viewed from an external position based on countless factors. In many cases, as with other art forms, we can generalize the good from the bad, keeping in mind that there are still critics of Don McLean's timeless classic "American Pie."

As you delve into this book, I am hopeful that you will assimilate the pages in the way you would gaze up at the Mona Lisa, perched on what appears to be a far larger wall than deserving of her unexpectedly minuscule proportions. You may love her smile. Perhaps you may see no smile at all, it doesn't matter. What matters is that you contemplate her through your lens, that you allot yourself the time and presence of mind to formulate whatever mental synapse you choose. Then when you step through the echoing halls of the marvelous Louvre, with Miss Mona's smile, or lack of, fading off in the distance, know that she has _impacted_ you with an opinion. In a universal sense, her brief interaction with you has impacted your interpretation of future artistic creations that retrace the same neural pathways that were ignited when you gazed upon her. You can never unsee her, unlearn her. You can never discard the impact of those fleeting moments. They have shaped you, to some minuscule or monumental degree, forever.

An Ordinary Artist

This, my readers, is fatherhood; and to the children in your lives, you are the da Vinci. An ordinary artist, you create a remarkable imprint with every note, each brush stroke and all manipulations of the soft palatable clay that lays itself into your hands daily. With a little effort, you will create a masterpiece. My words are not truth, rather contemplations for you to absorb. My suggestions are not scientific fact; rather bluesy riffs for you to hear, interpret, and then replay in your own musical interpretation. You see, some of us like Neil Diamond's original version of "Girl, You'll Be A Woman Soon"; and others of us like what Urge Overkill did with the tune. Either way, it's the same song, each with its own artistic take imprinted on it. Take my words and make them yours, you're the artist.

Chapter 1

Seven Very Memorable Words

Paint By Numbers

San Antonio, Texas is hot! There's really no way around it. You can taste the heat as the moisture in the air condenses in the back of your throat with every breath, and the humidity creates a blanket of sweat over your skin that refuses to evaporate and provide cooling relief. As a tourist this heat is tolerable. You wear shorts and a tank top every day as you stroll the Riverwalk, wind your way to find a conspicuous relic in The Alamo (sitting like an ancient memory engulfed in a modern wonderland), and then head off to the pool for some refreshing relaxation. Yup, in that mode it's very tolerable. It's when you have to strap on those boots, blouse those pants, button up that BDU (Battle Dress Uniform, a complex military term for a shirt), and put on that cover (another unnecessary play on words for what the normal world calls a hat), that heat becomes a little less tolerable.

I was 25 years old when I entered the United States Air Force, and like hundreds of thousands before me, San Antonio was where I was indoctrinated to life as an Airman. Ten miles south of San Antonio's Riverwalk, Lackland Air Force base hosts a number of military training schools, but nestled in the middle of them, and what it is best known for, is its role as the only Enlisted Basic Military Training for the Air Force. The basic training area is tucked away in its own space, separate from all of the inhabitants of the base that have already completed this grueling task. However, at times, during the grueling weeks of isolation from the outside world and consistent "correction" from your wonderful drill instructors, you could catch a glimpse of people walking normally, without straight arms and clenched fists and not squaring their corners[1]. Those brief moments would

---

[1] a requirement in basic training is to march everywhere you go, producing sharp ninety degree turns at every corner; this is termed squaring your corners

always remind you that soon this will end, and life will return to normal, or at least somewhat, because the reality was this decision, this adventure, would change my life as it has for the multitude of men and women that signed on the dotted line during a time when America was about to endure one of its longest wars. The year was 2002, and just a year before 4 planes had made 4 fateful trips, and our lives had changed forever.

The majority of people that enter into our armed services do so at a young age; eighteen to twenty years old and driven by a lifelong ambition to follow in a father's or grandfather's footsteps. Or possibly lost in a world of confusion and uncertainty about their future and looking for meaning in their lives. Military recruiters can spot those as easy as an eagle spots a vulnerable prey. And some, like me, found this path out of a sense of duty following a terrible set of events. Regardless of how we got there, here we were, and we were going through this together.

Being one of the older men in my squadron made it quite interesting. Immediately because of my age I was put into a leadership role. Some flourished in that role and some quickly were replaced by more competent leaders as the time went on. As the author of this book I am in the position to say that I most certainly excelled! Truth? Maybe, but it would take a bit of work on your part to prove otherwise, so good luck searching my Facebook, LinkedIn and other social media to find like connections that may know the answer to that question. Let me know how you make out.

Basic training was difficult. I finished first in my class, and I would still say that it was difficult. I often look upon those that try to proclaim otherwise with skepticism. As I stated, I was older and established when I enlisted. I had earned my B.A. from Rollins College in Winter Park, Florida, had a good career in the mental health field, and was flipping houses on the side. Life was good for me and having my freedom stripped away and enduring the "break you down to build you back up" process is taxing for the most mentally and physically prepared individuals. I had pride in many of my accomplishments up until this point, but marching across the parade field at Lackland, weighing in at a lean 145 pounds, I felt a sense of accomplishment unlike anything before.

The parade field is enormous, and on graduation day, when your family hasn't seen you for weeks, and graduates frequently look quite different than they did when they left, it has an air of excited anticipation that cuts through the oppressive humidity and creates a beating in your heart you are sure the man next to you can hear. The field is framed by full-size decommissioned aircraft, including a B-52 Stratofortress, F-4 Phantom II, SR-71 Blackbird, B-29 Superfortress, C-121 Constellation, B-17 Flying Fortress and a B-25 Mitchell. These planes, along with the pomp and circumstance and marching parade of graduation, generate a memorable experience for all involved. On that day, as I marched with my squadron past the bleachers with rows and rows of family, friends and loved ones squinting for a glimpse of the newly anointed Airman, I saw them; my mother, father ,and future ex-wife[2].

My mother is a dynamic woman, and that, my friends, is the understatement of the book. My family is all Italian and my mother exudes everything you would expect with that stereotype. Sunday dinners are a

---

[2] More on her later. For now, suffice it to say I am sure the pain I have is shared by many of the readers and is perhaps why this book is in your hands right now.

must. I will never be capable of making a decision without her telling me her "opinion" of that decision; and God forbid you wrong her, because she will remind you of it up until she or you takes their last breath. It will, however, be you that goes first because she always gets the last word! Now, yes, all those characteristics are true, but more than that, my mother impacts lives and makes change. That stubborn Italian woman never accepts a wrong. No matter how much the rest of the world tells her to let it go, those words simply fuel her drive to rally support and impact change. A characteristic of which I have always been envious. More to that point later.

The individual sitting next to her on that day was my father, and for one brief second we caught eyes. He was looking at me with that same simple smile that he always had and once again I wondered like so many times before what he was thinking. Unlike my mom you almost never knew what my father was thinking. He's a quiet man, but because of that, has always carried a weight to his words when he did speak. I have always been envious of that too! I learned many lessons in my life from that. Lessons that I didn't get until later years in reflection on the events. As a parent now, I realize how hard it is to hold back when you want to just grab your children, point them in the right direction, and scream, "Trust me damn it! I know what is best for you". My father held that back throughout my entire life, and yes again, I am envious because I struggle often to replicate that pattern.

After our procession, we marched back to our starting points, were anointed as official Airmen, and were finally allowed to see those who had come to watch us graduate. As I approached him, the reaction was predictable. From my mother came a tear-filled hug and thorough examination of my body as if she was looking to see if I was in one piece both mentally and

13

physically. From my dad came that quiet smile with a pat on the back and something to the effect of "Hey buddy", as if I had just seen him yesterday and hadn't just spent two months of isolation away from him.

Once we were set free, we were allowed a few hours with our family that afternoon. I gave them all a tour of our barracks, and realized that as impactful it was to me, to them it was just a large room with bunk beds aligned in an almost eerie symmetry.   Experiences elicit feelings, and at that moment my   flood of emotions differed heavily from theirs because of the experience of the last two months. From there we toured the base and eventually found a tucked away gazebo, abutting the woods. There we talked about my experiences; they got me up to speed on current events I had missed (most upsetting was the despicable season the New England Patriots had following their amazing 2001 Super Bowl run), and we just enjoyed each other's company. We had a pass to leave base the next day with our family, but for today, this was all we would get.

Eventually time ran out, and I had to go back to my dorm. My mom repeated her initial teary kisses and complete health check as if she was my primary care physician, and then my dad hugged me good-by. My dad got everyone in the car, closed their doors, and walked around the front of the blue Toyota Corolla rental (it's amazing the details you remember with significant events) and before he opened his door, he stopped, looked at me, and said 7 words. Words I will never forget. Words despite all my accomplishments I had never heard before. With his hand on the door handle he looked me in the eyes and said, "Brian, I am really proud of you."

Just a Bit More About Me

In terms of polar opposites, if Tom Brady lies on one end of the global popularity scale where everybody knows his name and face, I am on the exact opposite of that balance beam. Nobody knows who the hell I am. I relish that anonymity as I am a true introvert, masquerading as an extrovert in social constructs. As a result, I want to give you a little slice of me in the most compact version possible so we can then move on and get into the good shit. When my editor advised me to expand this section of the book, I had absolute writer's block. Of the countless stories, life events, and things about me I could tell, which should I choose? Where should I start? I was frozen, paralyzed by this last minute addition that I really didn't want to write. It's like getting to the finish line of a marathon, grabbing the Gatorade, hugging your spouse.....and then being told to go do another mile. Fuck off!

Here is what you will get. A few years ago I was asked to write a biographical summary to be listed in a pamphlet for a seminar I was speaking at. Thus, thank you cut and paste...here it is....told in the 3rd person narrative.

Brian LaFauci was born in Smithfield, Rhode Island on Dec 27th 1976 to two of the most wonderful parents a child could ask for, John and Joan LaFauci. In April of 1981, his life was ruined by the addition of his sister Ashlee. Just kidding, my sister is my best friend; love her mucho! Anyway, pressing on. Brian graduated from Smithfield High in 1994 and went on to attend Quinnipiac University and then Rollins College where he graduated with a Psychology major with a focus on Medical Studies. From there Brian received his Masters in Clinical School Psychology from Rhode Island College.

Paint By Numbers

Brian LaFauci began his professional career in 1999 as a School Psychologist for children and adolescents with a myriad of developmental disabilities at The Eleanor Briggs School in Warwick RI. With his clinical career in full swing, Brian followed a long time desire to serve our country and joined the RI Air National Guard. He enlisted in 2002 and was eventually commissioned as a Personnel Officer and ended his career after 11 years of service as an Aircraft Maintenance Officer. During this time Brian was activated for 18 months to run the deployment process for the RI Air National Guard during the heaviest period of our recent war fighting activities. This experience further developed Brian's leadership style, logistical skill set and knowledge of human resource systems.

Brian's successes in uniform resulted in him being hired for a number of Federal Veteran based programs including Executive Director of the RI Employer Support of the Guard and Reserve (ESGR), Executive Director of the RI Hero2Hire Program and New England Director of the Veteran Business Outreach Centers for the SBA.

In conjunction with his professional career, Brian has always had an entrepreneurial spirit. Brian co-founded a real estate investment corporation that is about to celebrate its 16 year anniversary, has a business consultant company, and owns and operates an indoor/outdoor sports facility in Seekonk, Massachusetts.

Despite being very career focused, Brian's time management puts two things first; family and community. Brian lives with his amazing wife Lori, who supports every bit of the craziness listed above, and their Brady Bunch family of 5 kids. Brian takes every opportunity to be an involved father which was an obvious catalyst to this book. Some of his passions are traveling, sports, nature, music, cigars and Liverpool FC, because we never walk alone!

So now that you know me so very well, let's get into the book!

What You Can Expect

This book will aim to do a few things very well:

Thing 1: Provide you with a number of stories and anecdotes that will make you laugh, cry, love and hate. It will be some Forest Gump type shit!

Thing 2: Provide you with a series of 8 Operations that you can implement into your life to help guide your efforts as a father, coach, teacher, role model, Deity, or whatever the hell you chose to use for your pronoun.

Thing 3: Put some cash money into my pocket. Thanks for buying the book!

Chapter 2

Who Gives a Shit

Paint By Numbers

Whenever you read a book, a part of what is imprinted on you is the personality of the author. It's inevitable, and can be disseminated in overt or subtle cues throughout the text. What you will clearly identify with me is that I swear. I do it often, emphatically, and with pride. There was a period of time where this was frowned upon, and those that used profanity were viewed as less intelligent or lacking in emotional control. Fuck that. Research now shows quite the opposite, and if you would like to take a fun subject like swearing and make it boring as shit, look at the research. Otherwise, you can just take my word for it. I mean let's think about this for a minute; if my swearing is an identifier that I lack intelligence to convey my thoughts appropriately and you still paid money for this book, then that would be quite an indictment on your intelligence, correct? Thus, for the sake of both you and me, we will call that myth bullshit and press on.

Who, therefore, gives a shit about my dad; and that one moment we had together; and how impactful it was? In my estimation we all should, because embedded in that comment was a concept that is severely lacking across our country right now. The bottom line is this: be it father, uncle, big brother, or any other paternal role that exists in our society; strong, positive male role models are far too rare; and the results are devastating. The sociological factors leading to this stem from many different areas that we will examine in this book. You can find astounding numbers of fathers who walk away from their duties for innumerable reasons. Those that choose drugs, alcohol, or other addictions over their children. Ones that find their gratification in their daily work and thus find little time for their sons or daughters. Contrarily, there are some who wish to be involved yet lack in the ability or confidence to do so effectively.

In other aspects, sometimes struggling to be a positive male role model has nothing to do with any of the above circumstances. Outside influences affect many of us. Court systems often still adopt a 1950's philosophy on equal time and visitation rights for fathers, and thus many fathers are immediately treated as less worthy in split households. Ironically, if the same pattern occurred between two people of differing race it would make front page news. However, when it's between a father and mother, the courts seem blind to this disparity of treatment. Economic situations frequently require dual parent incomes with many fathers and mothers working second jobs to simply support their families, all while minimizing time with the children.

Even more prominent in recent years are fathers who have left their kids for extended periods of time to serve their country during this seemingly endless war. To be honest, it really doesn't matter to me with what category you identify. My goal in this book is not to create a list of all the reasons we could suck as male role models. It's to provide a framework for all of us to get better. To assist us men in identifying the importance of the issue and how to find ways to be involved. But most importantly, not just involved, involved with purpose; because do you know who gives a shit more than us? The children do.

In this book I promise not to tell a multitude of stories to conceptualize each point. In my opinion that would get quite dull, and the one thing I hate in some authors is the replacement of quality for quantity. If my book, therefore, is a bit shorter than you expected, it's because I believe that with one good story, you will get the point. The tough part for me will be choosing which stories to tell. You see, I am not simply a divorced father of two who faces these challenges daily; I was also a mental health clinician for many years and witnessed staggering patterns in relation to paternal involvement and emotional development in children. Now let me qualify that statement. I am certainly no Florence Nightingale (for those of you that don't know, Florence Nightingale was a famous nurse and statistician, member of the Royal Statistical Society and just a really, really smart woman). However, I can say with a significant amount of confidence, there is one observable pattern I've seen over and over again: kids with shitty dads often are a little fucked up. The boy we will refer to as Jimmy came from this dynamic, and yes, he was .... you get it. (See, I also know when I am swearing too much).

You don't get into counseling psychology for the money. Nobody ever, ever said to me in my journey, "Hey, want to be rich? You should get your graduate degree in counseling psychology and then just ride the road to riches!" Yea, that comment has never been uttered by any human, in any country, during any time in history. Never! You do it because helping people always feels good. Even for people who often chose not to help people; I challenge them to tell me it didn't feel good during those few times they did. For me it was children I enjoyed helping most. I felt they deserved it. Often they were thrust into a situation by pure shit luck, and forced to face challenges that would make even the strongest adults explode in anger when the weight of hopelessness became too heavy. Working to provide them a future with hope was extremely rewarding, and Jimmy needed hope. Jimmy needed a lot, but hope was very much right there at the top.

Jimmy knew who his father was. Often times I found this worse. You can disguise reality to a child who never met or knew his or her father. You can blame their lack of involvement on a number of things that are somewhat easy for a child to absorb. We could list the excuses, but again, quality over quantity here. However, a dad who is in and out of a child's life; reliable on some days, and unreliable on many others; that kind of father is extremely hard for a child to process. Jimmy had that kind of dad. To make it worse, often women who chose shitty men, chose another shitty man, and another, and another. Yup, not Miss Nightingale, but it's a pattern I have seen enough to believe. Jimmy had that kind of mom too.

Jimmy was angry! Now I have kids, and I assume most of you do too. All our kids can get angry, but Jimmy was really angry. For those of you who have never really worked with, parented, or known a child like Jimmy, let me explain what angry looked like. If you key into human behavior a lot, there are always precursors to a person just exploding. As a school clinician it was my job to pay exceptionally close attention to these cues in order to intervene and help overt disaster. With Jimmy I became very good at seeing the cues and it always started with his word choice and inflection. In a good mood, Jimmy would answer most yes or no questions with a well enunciated "esss" at the end of his yes and an equally enunciated "oh" when responding in the negative, clear as day, as if raised in the most proper of all English speaking homes.

On these good days there was a glint in his eyes of hope, and at times even an air of pride in his academic work or good behavior for that day. I would do everything I could to embrace those moments with Jimmy. To allow this boy, now smiling, talking to me in a relaxed tone, the opportunity to prolong this feeling for as long as I could. Kids deserve those moments, periods where their guard is completely down because they are entirely trusting of the situation they are in with you and allow themselves to be vulnerable.

23

For me I think of the times I tickle or wrestle my little boy and how he completely lets himself go in those moments, knowing always that when he has had enough he can trust for me to quit. Jimmy did not have that experience of trust with men and that was evident in how infrequently he would allow himself to be vulnerable.

Now, those were the good days. However, on the not-so-good days, and they were frequent, Jimmy's emotional meltdown could always be first identified through his apparent relocation to South Boston where the audible "esss" was replaced with an elongated and muffled "ehhhhh", and the equally as distinguishable "oh" reverted to an un-emphatic "nahhh". In those moments, there would be no vulnerability. In those moments Jimmy would defend himself mentally, emotionally, and physically with the will and vigor of those men, who so valiantly defended the Alamo, before it was an ancient relic in a bustling city.

That was it. It was that simple, and as soon as you heard it, you knew that it wouldn't be long before the years of pent-up frustration, anger and instability would rear its evil head. "Here's Jimmy!" (Insert image here of Jack Nicholson's head, squeezed between the hole in the bathroom door, which he created with an axe as the glint of craziness shines in his eyes). Oh yea, that was Jimmy, without the axe of course, or else we would have done a pretty poor safety check that day! In the same fashion a Bugatti Chiron goes from 0-60; Jimmy went from a slight inflection change to a physical danger to anyone who was in the radius of a thrown desk in the blink of an eye. (For all non-car enthusiasts, the Bugatti Chiron is an extreme luxury sport car, boasting 1500 horsepower, a top speed of over 250 mph, and can be yours for the low introductory price of $2.6 million American dollars).

At times, I would question if Jimmy contained the same amount of horsepower when pushed over the thin line of his breaking point. What always amazed me was the strength, resolve, and desire to destroy anyone or anything in front of him Jimmy displayed in his fits of rage. At times it makes you angry that this boy, whom you are trying desperately to help, wishes such harm on you. Then, inevitably, the crazed glint in his eye would serve as a magic ball, and the cloudy swirling chaos would give way to the true underlying sadness that was driving the behavior. In those moments I was always engulfed in sadness, knowing how hard it was going to be to erase all the damage that had been done. Almost always, when the exhaustion finally set in, and he could fight no more, Jimmy would cry. He would cry hard.

It was no coincidence that Jimmy had little tolerance for being told what to do. Do you know from whom Jimmy really hated to be told something? You got it, men! From all the men that came into Jimmy's life, (or didn't come into his life for that matter) Jimmy had learned one thing: that men are untrustworthy; and to a child there are few characteristics less damning than adults who cannot be trusted. Men often left his life. Why? He didn't know, but he sure as hell assumed he had something to do with it. Over time, unfortunately, Jimmy learned that regardless of the reason, men will leave him, and it hurt too much when it happened. Except, if he just made them hate him; and if he just hated them (or at least convinced himself he did) then it was so much easier when they left. Jimmy tried to get me to hate him for four years straight, until finally, one day, for no apparent reason, he gave up.

It took four long years, five days a week, seven hours a day, with countless one-on-one therapy sessions, thousands of hours of peer group therapy, a whole bunch of medication changes, and a very resilient; therapeutic and academic team. Four long years before Jimmy finally learned that he could trust one man: me. That was something we could build on. After that point, Jimmy was a different kid; at least when he was around me. He would let me help, trusted my advice, and began to learn how to work through his anger and control his outbursts. It's interesting how long it takes to get used to this. I had a college friend who, every time I saw him, would try to slap my nuts; and I mean every time. Twenty years out of college now and that flinch reaction is still there. The nut slap hasn't happened for years, (although it may now that I have resurrected it with this book), but the reaction remains. With Jimmy it was tough to get to the point of believing there were no more outbursts, that the vulnerability was there for good, and that he was actually heeding advice and trusting some guidance. Those were good life moments for both Jimmy and me.

Who gives a shit? You better, because the reality was that with the right male role model, Jimmy would have never had to endure 4 years of hell. Not his fault at all. I can tell you hundreds of "Jimmy" stories, all with their own unique aspects. Each one with slightly different characteristics as to how they got there and how they react when triggered, but they all are identical in one way, and by now you get what that is. That is why it is time to man up, and avert the paternal crisis.

Let's face another reality here, and that pink elephant in this chapter is the fact that a majority of our children are not Jimmy's. For the most part, they are functioning on a fairly normal basis, existing among the children of today in a fairly inconspicuous manner. What then is the problem? If most children are getting through school, going on to jobs, living "normal" lives, how are there any problems at all? The following chapters will serve to outline these issues and the operations we as men can take to have our positive impact upon them.

Paint By Numbers

Chapter 3

The Ordinary Sculptor - A Way Forward

The chapters thus far have been a journey down time immemorial, a discussion of actions, dossiers, and anecdotes which have already occurred. While I strongly believe we learn from the past, I am also inclined to believe that the purpose of this book should provide a roadmap for a way forward. A set of actions, or virtues for that matter, to guide us as fathers and male role models for the betterment of our children and the future generations. There are eight of them for that matter, and I will refer to them as operations. Eight operations.

Why eight you say.....because its my fucking book........thats why. I left a few blank pages at the end for any of you who feel I should have made 10 or 11 or maybe 23 suggestions because you are infatuated with basketball and feel the only great number is 23! I dropped that in there for all my ballers...the rest of you are straight lost and just got tripped up by my nasty vernacular crossover. Slam the Dunk baby!

Ok, quick anecdote here. I am a Providence College, PC, as they are affectionately referred to here in good old Rhody season ticket holder. They play their home games at the Dunkin Donuts Center. Yea, I know, shocker! Any-who, that Cathedral of basketball greatness is affectionately referred to as "The Dunk". Therefore, whenever PC breaks out for an obvious dunk, I stand up and yell "Slam the Dunk", adding the unnecessary article into the middle as a witty play on the fact that we are at "The Dunk" and the player is about to perform a "Slam Dunk". For a few years now I have tried, unsuccessfully, to get my surrounding fellow ticket holders to join in my obviously hilarious cheer. I can say with absolute certainty that should this book become a complete failure, but, the "Slam the Dunk" chant gains some legs from it, all will have been worthwhile.

SLAM THE DUNK!

Ok, anecdote terminated, back to the eight guiding principles. The challenge faced with only eight guiding principles was the complexity of life situations and challenges that create varying capacities, abilities and reasonable implementations for the reader. With this dynamic, the recommendations are not presented in any specific order. Any number of them implemented with programmed regularity would be beneficial to the children or adolescents in your life. My recommendation would be to challenge yourself to do a little more than what's easy, or what you feel you may be already doing. Regardless of motivation or situation, the end goal in this game of paternal prodigiousness can only be two-fold: the current and future interconnection between you and the child, and to provide the developmental support all children require from a male role model. Depending on the nature of the relationship, the duration of the interactions can vary greatly. In one setting a father may spend years with a child and have countless opportunities to implement the suggestions provided. Others may be operating on limited time, as caregivers, mentors, educators, coaches, or a myriad of other roles in which a child views a paternal figure in his or her life as a guiding beacon.

To further this concept, think about the men in your life that shepherded you through various life stumbling-blocks. Many times a father would be the image to quickly materialize in the mind's eye when recalling the life lessons imparted on us by others. Think about the sit-down talk after your first fight with a friend, or the encouragement provided following the news that you didn't make the varsity baseball team. The neuron pathways that recall that event would almost certainly be intertwined with the memories of dad, or the figurative "dad" that stood in that role during that time. Regardless of the relationship, it was the advice, at that precise moment, that created a teachable instance and helped to shape future behavior for a young child. Unless it didn't! In many cases, without that paternal guidance, these life events remain trapped in the developing mind of a young child or adolescent, swimming around in a simplistic maze where experienced life events have yet to break down hedgerows leading to vastly more complex interpretations and understandings of the event; and most importantly, the way forward following that event. The differential factor here is simple; at those key moments in our life, was there any male guidance or was that placeholder left void?

As children, we don't fall and stumble once, and we certainly don't learn the first time.....or the second or third in my case. It takes countless repetition of failure, and countless repetition of support following failure to make notable change. Therefore, as a father figure, we need to be present as much as possible to help our children break down those hedgerows of limited knowledge, expand understanding of the world, and the successful ways to navigate within its complexity.

If at this point you are still not sold on the importance of this, and your thick skull can't absorb the amazing knowledge I am dropping right now, I will hit you with this mic drop and then you can turn the page! In an article from Marketresearch.com in Feb of 2018, the life-coaching industry topped 1 billion dollars in revenue in 2018 and is expected to hit $1.34 billion by 2022. That's a whole lot of grown adults that are paying a shit ton of money for other people to provide them guidance on life decisions. Fair to assume that if they are paying for it, then they don't have much of it readily available in their life. When I need male guidance, I ask my dad, or a myriad of other male role models I have in my life. Below are eight operations to help you be the man you aspire to be. Time to man up gentlemen!

Paint By Numbers

Chapter 4

Why Call Them Operations

When I think about an operation I envision a process that involves planning, thought, modification, execution and reflection. In a nutshell that's what parenting and mentoring is and exactly what these eight executions are meant to be. In each one of these I have succeeded splendidly and in each one experienced immense failure. I am sure you will experience the same. There have been instances where the immediate implementation was met with adversity and complaints from my children. "Noooooooooooooowwwah Daaaaahd"is the most annoying fucking thing in the world to hear when you have put time and effort into planning out time with your children. Those two simple words which are often articulated with the emulated pitch of Steven Tyler singing "Walk this Way" have pushed my anger meter to the point of combustion. Had my frontal lobe not engaged at that exact moment the reaction would be tantamount to the end scene in Once Upon a Time...In Hollywood. I would sick my 125-lb trained attack dog on one of my poor children while then bashing the other one to a bloody mess. Fucked up scene, isn't it! Thank you frontal lobe, I heart you!

Anyway, an operation is made to have flexibility and to be evaluated post-execution for successes, failures, and lessons learned. Use these eight operations in that way, and chart the course best for you to be successful in their execution on future occasions. If you get the ever dreaded "Noooooooooooooowwwah Daaaaahd", then ask them why? You will find that the conversation will provide you clarity and focus for planning the next operation.

Why Call Them Operations

Operation 1

Get it on the Calendar

Paint By Numbers

Ok, ready to feel like a real asshole? Take a break from the book for a minute and go into whatever calendar you use to schedule your life. Great, now scroll through the events you have going on: Lunch with Dave, Conference Call with Employee Morale Team, Dentist Appointment for cavity fill. All in all, there is some really stupid insignificant shit on there isn't there? Fast forward to your funeral.........now look at your calendar again..........how many of the people on there in the last month would say a few words about you at your funeral? Even better, how many of them would even go to your depressing, tuxedo dressed, cold body viewing? Fucked up isn't it!

As I was engaged in the writing of this book, a friend of mine passed away at the ripe age of 99. Frank Tedesco, or as he was known to those who had the pleasure to be impacted by him, Lieutenant Frank Tedesco was a B24 Liberator pilot in WWII. Frank's military and civilian accomplishments are extensive, and deserve more than a brief mention in this book. However, in honor of his legacy I will impart you with a few stories.

To set the stage, it is imperative to revisit a few or those damn statistics I promised to not revisit a chapter or two ago. In World War II, the survival rate of the bomber crews was just under 45%, and the chance of being captured was just under 8%. If you struggle at math like I do, I will save you the use of the calculator. That's a greater than 53% chance that if you went out on a mission you would be either shot down or captured. With each and every mission, Frank had a better chance of not returning home than on completing his mission.........and he proceeded to fly 35 of these missions throughout the war.

While battling the mental demons that would naturally haunt any of us facing such odds, Frank and all of his fellow pilots battled unheated and unpressurized cockpits at altitudes that frequently experienced temperatures below zero degrees. With oxygen masks affixed to their face, pilots would often have to defrost the frozen masks upon returning to base in order to remove them. Frozen, battling unsettling odds, rattling in the cockpit from the impact of anti-aircraft guns, Frank fearlessly pressed on, destroying priceless German supply lines and fuel depots; efforts that would ensure Allied success in the war.

A few years before his passing, over a dinner with Frank and our family, following a rendition of one of his favorite tunes from the 1940's (Yes, this son of a bitch could still sing at 95 years old!), Frank gave us a gift. The type of gift the infamous Dr. Suess would reference in one of his most famous children's novels; "It came without tags. It came without packages, boxes or bags. And he puzzled and puzzled 'till his puzzler was sore. Then the Grinch thought of something he hadn't before". Frank gave a gift of the heart, and conveyed the gift without knowledge or intent.

Absent of any comment, Frank walked over to an old wooden cupboard, sitting unlit in the corner of the small, unpretentious coastal home, in which we had just enjoyed dinner. From the cupboard, he pulled out an old photo album, worn in a way that clearly displayed it had spent years in an area where moisture, mold and mildew had faded and discolored it to its current state, an appearance expected for a stagnant fixture in a coastal home.

He opened the album with the sticky sound of plastic releasing its moisture formed grip from connected pages, revealing photos which visually appeared as if altered with one of many instagram filters, yet the fading and discoloration was clearly organic. As Frank sat down, he gestured to the children to come closer and at that very moment, a silence fell over the room as the thick air of anticipation weighed on all of us. With the glimpse of the first photo displaying what was clearly a cratered landscape, the aftermath of a devastating bomber run, I felt a lump rise up in my throat and a quickening of my heart rate. I knew what was about to transpire. The children, despite having no idea of the gravity of the interaction they were about to be part of, seemed to sense the same significance of the situation.

Perhaps it was a keen recognition of the grown-up response, or another intuitive perception that children seem to magically possess. Whatever it was, it was real, and in that moment, everyone in the room knew something special was about to happen.

Page by page, conscious recollections were spilled out, creating vivid imagery for the spectators in that room on that cool summer's evening. Animated details were described, providing all of us with the firsthand experiences of the greatest generation. A man 95 years of age, shared a story with all of us in the manner and detail in which many of us would describe our workday. It was as if 65 years had been merely a blip on the memorial radar. As impressive as the retrospective accuracy was, the apogee of the evening came from the children's ability to transpose the textbook education they had received up until that point into a real life understanding of personal sacrifice. In that very moment I watched my children grow a respect, admiration and appreciation for Frank, and for those that served in that great war.

Upon leaving Frank's wake and saying goodbye to his family, I spoke with my children about his passing. My relationship with Frank was a short one in relation to the 99 years he spent on this earth. I had about ten get-togethers with him through a period of about 6 years. My children had even less contact. Despite that, the moments that he imparted on them were impactful enough that his passing left a scar on them and on me as well.

I am not Frank's son, but this book isn't just about fathers, it's about the importance of men in the lives of children at the right times to create lasting memories. Frank put me on his calendar, and in doing so provided myself and my family with experiences we will never forget. In those days and hours we spent with him we learned fearlessness, humility, commitment to a cause greater than oneself, and ultimately the fragility of life no matter how much of a superhuman the subject appears to be. Frank put me and my family on his calendar and as a result I was there at the end of his life. He imprinted values in us that will last a lifetime. I am eternally thankful for that.

With the children in our lives that we are trying to guide and develop, their are many ways which you can lock in time with them. The first thing that I do is break out certain days of the week that my kids are blocked in on my calendar. As a divorced father with joint custody I am with my children for two of the weekdays every week (Monday through Tuesday) and then every other weekend (Friday through Monday). During that set time I always have that time blocked off on my calendar as unavailable for work.

In order to make this work, since my separation I have made sure to select employment decisions, whether they be as a traditional employee, or in the self-employed capacity that I am now, to ensure that any time I am with my kids I am fully available for them. Trust me in that I am fully aware of the fortunate nature of this situation, and my wife and other members of my family make sacrifices of their time with me in order to make this happen. I pull early morning and late nights to make sure I am giving my business everything it needs, and I work my other obligations around my time with them. For many of you this may be very difficult, and for those of you coming at this from an intact family, there are many other scheduling actions you can take to get your kids on the calendar. To add clarity to this, I want to paint the picture of what that reality looks like. First, let me outline what it does not look like. I do not follow my children around the house observing their every action. I do not force them into 12 hours a day of time with their dad. Over-parenting is a problem that we can delve into later.

When I put my kids on the calendar, I am making myself available for them should they need me and adding in appropriate levels of time and activities to do with them based on their age range. With my 12-year-old son, I have the luxury of still being a desired source of time and entertainment, second only to the time he spends shooting up his friends on Fortnite. With my 14 year old daughter, an hour of time is a precious commodity which would remove her from the most important aspect of her life, her friends. With my older stepchildren ages 21-27, my time with them is much more fluid as they have created their own lives and we fit in time based on shared interests and experiences.

There is a good article written in Fatherly.com by Matthey Utley titled "How to Recognize the Three Stages of Adolescence Every Child Experiences". Whether you're experiencing this for the first time or are on your third or fourth child, give it a read. It's a wonderful reminder of what the children in our lives are going through. I chose the times I engage with my children appropriately in order to ensure they approach it excitedly to be with me.

Get it on the Calendar

To ensure success with this I recommend engaging with your children on things they enjoy as much as possible.....no matter how painful some may be. I play the video games my son enjoys a bit and I will connect with my daughter on the social media platform of her choice. These actions fall into the less formal, unstructured events we engage in together, opportunistic episodes, occurring predominantly out of the accomplishment of making ourselves available. Scheduling the availability begets the fortuity.

Workouts are another outstanding way to schedule activities to do with your children, and also have the obvious benefit of producing strapping, rock solid, physical specimens within your family lineage. This way, when the next apocalyptic event occurs, you have a self created warrior base with whom to go fuck shit up. Together, we train a couple times a week and these are times that both myself and my kids look forward to. Obviously, any healthy activity that can be incorporated into the time spent with our children is a worthwhile exercise. These workouts fall more into the category of scheduled family time events, and these are as important as the unstructured spontaneous interactions we create by simply being available for our children.

In addition to the aforementioned advantages of exercise, there are supplementary benefits to exercising with your kids. These benefits, while often concealed by the prominence of the actual act of working out, are primarily what drives the billion dollar industry that is group exercise. Bring yourself to the end of a cross-fit, high intensity interval training, spin, or whatever exercise modality you choose. If, at this point, I have lost you, then add to your list of action items to get your ass into shape.

Continuing on, revert your mind's eye to the moment the class has ended. The instructor, a beautiful, dark haired woman, graciously wipes the beads of glistening sweat off of her hardened tanned physique. As the cool down music slowly reverberates throughout the studio, sounds of heavy breathing slowly returning to their natural cadence, filling the muffled silence between the music notes. "Great job everyone" echoes the instructor's voice over the speakers. "I'll see all of you next week". Scanning around the room you see the participants smiling and sharing an exhausted beam of accomplishment with each other. High fives, compliments, and comments of personal success are shared throughout as the group makes its way to embark on their daily vocations. The communal feeling of accomplishment binds the group in the same manner that survivors of traumatic events are fated together.

The innate beauty of engaging in events, that can cause the body physical or mental pain, has been shown in research to create a sort of "social bonding" between the participants. That connection has also been shown to increase compatibility, bonding and camaraderie among the individuals. For those of us who know how difficult it can be to attain that status with a hormonal, know-it-all, smart ass teenager, I'll take any option I can get. To help get my kids engaged I have a series of 40 workout exercises on these cards and I let them pick some of the ones they want to do that day. Then we go through a series of workouts for about 30 minutes together, supporting and challenging each other the whole way. Go get after it! Bring those kids into your workout routines and get to the bonding.

In addition to workouts, there are other invaluable actions you can take to get your children on your calendar. Included in them are two of my favorites, vacations and meals! ...I can hear some of you now. Wait, hold on you pretentious asshole, did you just say vacations and meals? Ok, meals I can see, but vacations? So you're telling me to connect with my kids I need to drop $10,000 on the god forsaken hell of Disney Parks every year? Hold on there cowboy, just hear me out. I have a family of 7 so I am the most cost conscious vacationer there is. Let's get to that one in a minute. Let's start by looking at meals.

Traditionally, in most American households, it would be fair to say we consume an average of 3 meals a day. Five, for those of you who subscribe to the small meal intake protocol. Some of you may even partake in the ever popular, fast until noon and then only eat from noon until 6pm. Even more of you may be on a bacon only diet. Ok, I made that one up (or maybe it does exist, who knows). Regardless, we can all come to an agreement that dietary habits in our country combined with insane schedules of work, life, kids sports, activities and all the other bullshit we cram into a 24 hour day makes the decision as to scheduling a family meal a crucial one. When breaking down the meal most likely to be capable of consuming together, dinner usually wins out. On weekends, however, that meal may shift to being breakfast depending on your various situations. Regardless of when they occur, how silent they can be at times, or how much push back you may get for them, planning meals together as a family is an absolute must. Get them on the calendar.

Vacations. I heard a wonderful quote once which said: "Take vacations, you can always find time to make money; you can't always find time to make memories". Then what defines a vacation? Most of us are limited by funds, time off, life events, and other barriers to making vacations a common occurrence, so here are my suggestions. First, just saying "we're going on vacation" makes us process the event differently than an ordinary day. Words have a mystifying way of initiating an ideological metamorphosis; turning what would otherwise be a humdrum Saturday into an extraordinary adventure. The simple act of taking a few days away, has a number of outstanding effects on interactions.

From the parent standpoint, getting away from the house, even if it's to the hotel an hour away, removes the drive to complete work, clean the house, and do the myriad of other activities that take away meaningful interactions with the kids. From a child standpoint, the new and exciting surroundings often promote increased exploration and conversation. Lastly, when it's just you and the kids, you all naturally become each other's entertainment. So head on out! Whether it's to the local campground an hour away, or halfway across the world, the impact of the time together is what is truly important and will occur regardless of the destination. Get those vacations on the calendar today!

Therefore, operation numero uno in this guide is to get these kids on your calendar. If I opened up my calendar right now I would have time with my kids absolutely blocked out. We are all busy, I have a real estate company, own and operate a 7 day a week sport complex, have started a few non-profits, provide business counseling support through my consultant company and I am writing this damn book. I'm as busy as a seven armed whore in a hand-job parlor. (Insert intentional pause here for you to laugh your ass off at that masterful sentence). Most importantly, I make sure my kids are on my schedule!

So for some of you, this operation will be crucial due to a separation or divorce within the family. That circumstance was mine as well and can be filled with turmoil and disruption for both the adults and the children. Using the calendar technique will help settle some of that turmoil for all parties involved. We all find ourselves in that situation for different reasons. I want to share my story with you, along with some suggestions from things I learned the hard way if any of you are currently in that same space.

When It All Falls Apart

Divorce was not a part of my upbringing. Outside of a couple of friends growing up, my parents and most of my surrounding peers had maintained an intact family, as did their parents and their parents and so on and so on. You just didn't give up or quit. That was always the message in my family growing up, and I was certain on that day that I took my wedding vows that as a believer in counseling and communication, there would be nothing we couldn't work through as a couple.

The world of marriage was to me a fraternity I was proud to be a part of, and the family I was about to create was the most important thing in my life. Even some of the subtle things, that many men would claim little concern for, were to me a valued part of my outward expression of commitment. I had purchased a very nice platinum and diamond engagement ring for my wife, and would frequently joke at how the men get the raw end of the deal on that transaction.

Despite my frequent jabs, I did view this purchase as worthy of the commitment I was prepared to undertake, and thus the price tag was quite hefty for a young man with a career in the non-lucrative mental health field. Fortunately for me at this time I had already begun my real estate investment career and used the profits from a recent sale to complete the purchase. In turn, when the time came for me to purchase what would soon be the symbolic item to adorn my hand for what I believed would be the length of my life, I took equal stock in that purchase. I wanted a ring that would adequately represent my value of the commitment of marriage and thus settled on a scrolled white gold ring, embedded with 3 diamonds, and later adorned with the birthstones of my two children. It was a perfect representation of the family structure that I cherished, and despite constant ridicule from my friends to the somewhat ostentatious nature of it, I loved it and all that it symbolized.

Early in marriage, the two of us shared the many joyous adventures that young couples are supposed to share. My family, which has always been very close, embraced our marriage as I knew they would and it was wonderful to watch the family pictures on the walls in my childhood home grow in size and number as a new family was formed. There are so many stories of families that don't embrace one another. The horrific image of the evil mother-in-law battling to the death with her newly appointed daughter-in-law, who could never provide for her son the way she could. Fortunately for me, this was not the case, and aside from a few isolated arguments here and there, we were as close as any merged family could have been.

On my end, this merger was quite easy; my wife's mother had passed tragically when my wife was young, and her father (ironically and sadly) was never involved. Therefore, the extent of my interaction with her family was with her brother, who lived about 5 hours away and when we saw a few times a year, and her sister, whom we saw on a more regular basis. During holidays, we would frequently have all of us together, and since my mother loves a big holiday, this new dynamic was embraced and welcomed.

For all intents and purposes, our family had morphed together like two songs remixed into one. An intense rock classic, whose harmonic beat, when paired with the vocals of a poppy young female, makes you wonder how the two ever existed without one another. My side of the family provided the harsh undertone of AC/DC with the easily distinguished guitar riff of the classic song "Back in Black". With my family's Italian heritage, we are loud, opinionated, and love a good argument. Family dinners are often a volley of conversations, jockeying with one another for position; each one fighting to subdue the ambient noise of surrounding voices the way that Brian Johnson's voice elevates itself to compete with the blaring chords from guitarist Angus Young.

My ex-wife's family was softer in nature and thus seemed uncomfortable at first with this dynamic, but just like those harmonic remixes, managed to integrate their voices into our maniacal volley and with Angus' riffs bouncing off the walls, Alicia Keys fluidly harmonized among the noise. The end result was a dinner table filled with faces and sounds that appeared as if they had broken bread together for centuries. A conversation emanated that had the ease of a deep breath, effortlessly flowing in and out, and respiring life into the surroundings. I loved it; and even now, as we have integrated a new family, it is pure energy for me to be in these settings. With the amazing mash-up playing in the background, just when it would seem impossible for the song to be any better, in comes the high-pitched train whistle and low kick drum, and despite all conventional wisdom that these sounds would never mix, magically, they do. My two young children had miraculously blended into our orchestra in a seamless manner, leaving a top billboard hit that would spend ages on the charts.

At that moment, in all its harmonic glory, I could have never seen how the voice of Alicia Keys would slowly decay, leaving behind an off pitch and toneless vibrato that no longer synchronized in our orchestra. Turning points are so much more identifiable in hindsight and so discreetly masked in the moment.

The deterioration of the voice occurred in the same manner that an aged singer can no longer carry the elegant notes for the same duration or in the same octave. To the untrained listener, the song is still the same classic it was upon original release, and in most cases with human interactions, many of us are untrained listeners. This is not a jab at society, and in truth I fully include myself in that criticism. The reality is that to truly hear the music and to wholly understand an individual, you must immerse yourself in their every behavior, attend yourself to their words with a radar like sensitivity, and allow the combined information to come together and form what is true and honest about them.

The issue that we all face is that our interactions with almost everyone in our lives does not allow for that; thus we are revealed to only their desired self. The image that person chooses to present to the world, and in that perception, we are almost all studio recordings of "Stairway to Heaven". We hit every note, keep perfect time, and work harmonically with our fellow band members. Flawless. Seamless. Ideal. Complete. That is what we show to almost everyone we meet.

To truly listen to another human being, you must, through countless repetition sit in on all the jam sessions. Watch as instruments fail, voices crack, and time and measure are constantly off. It is only through endless experiences like this that we truly get to know someone. As a result, a common look of confusion and bewilderment emanated from our close friends and family when we explained to them that a marriage had failed. It is not their fault for this reaction; most of them had been listening to the studio recording of the relationship for years.

In the end, the song did not remain the same; and after years of counseling and countless hours of wondering what I could do next to fix this horrible relationship I was in, it happened. I decided that I could no longer live this way; but what I had not decided was if I was ready to abandon the ability to wake up to my children on a daily basis. There, in that state of purgatory, floating between the two things, that paradoxically brought me the greatest joy and the most intense anguish, lay a decision. One that more than likely you as the reader has faced, and struggle with possibly still. Now, with this decision far behind me, there are two stories that I can tell; what I did do, and what I would have done. I often wish we could live life twice, as so often these two things are rarely congruous.

What I did was inadvisable, as most things that are easy tend to be. I chose to wake up to my kids every morning because I felt justified in that action. Why should I have to give that up? After all, I had dumped all my efforts into years of counseling with little reciprocity from my partner. And simultaneously, I chose to find love. Why should I have to give that up either? I believed in my heart that my partner did not know what true love meant and I wanted that as part of my life, so I found it.

I lived this life for a very short period of time, and during that time, my emotional state was in such constant unrest that I was never truly enjoying either life I was living. In the end, my love for another woman became evident and I gave away all the control I had once had in the decision for my future. My desire to take the easy way out led to a much harder road going forward, provided my ex-wife with the ability to pin the marriage failure on my infidelity, and sparked anger from close friends and family. Epic fail!

If I had a do-over, here is how it would look, and here is my suggested list of steps for all of you, who are sitting in the same purgatory that plagued my life for over a year.

1) You must exhaust every aspect of counseling with your partner. Whether it be psychological, spiritual, holistic, or any other form upon which the two of you can agree. Set aside your preconceived notion that it's all bullshit. It's not! The only way for two people to fix a broken situation is through communicating what is at the heart of your frustration. That takes time. I recommend committing yourself to at least one year of counseling every other week to make any progress.[3]

2) Commit to being faithful during this process, you cannot commit to the tough task of relationship repair if the alternative is the ease of a "side-piece". In the end every one of those girls on the side will come with their own set of issues you will need to work through.

3) If your therapist doesn't suggest it, tell them you want actual "homework". When relationships go sour you need to reprogram activities in. Plus this will be a clear indicator if one person isn't doing his or her part.

4) Accept the fact that you are definitely partially to blame for the issues. Without that there is no chance.

5) Should all efforts fail, do not commit adultery! It will make the process of separation so much more difficult and create issues far outside of the realm of your relationship.

---

[3] We did go to counseling for 3 years. However, in the end, only one of us was completing the assigned work, and that doesn't work. Both parties must follow through.

6) Leave before you cheat. If after the year of counseling (or more if you were making progress), things are going badly then discuss separation. (Going back I would have left my wife and then began to see other people).

Operation 2:

Join a Fatherhood Group

Paint By Numbers

Organizational structures permeate our culture for discernible and poignant reasons. From our battlefront tactics and preparedness to our corporate framework, the billion-dollar industry of creating a stalwart union has proven its worth. Therefore, the same benefits afforded to the aforementioned are available to us as fathers and come with a myriad of benefits.

Guidance and direction come to us in two major vehicles, solicited and unsolicited. Depending on the timing, life events, and mind-state; either can be equally impactful; thus exposure to external sources of unsolicited guidance holds great importance in helping us on our fatherly journey. It is for this reason that the individuals and influence that surrounds us is so crucial to the direction we take.

In a venerable cemetery, tucked into the contemporary, bustling concrete jungle known as Brooklyn, New York, lies the weathered tombstones of two brothers. Clifton and William Prentiss, side by side as brothers should be in their eternal memorial. From a visitor, standing in the open-air breeze, which seems to permeate through all cemeteries, the image would conjure a belief of life long connectedness between the two. The voices from those graves would whisper a very different story. The real story shows us the impact a community can have on one's life and how impactful the individuals around us can be in charting our course.

In the mid to late 1830's, William and Clifton Prentiss were born just outside Baltimore, Maryland. A few years apart in age, Clifton forever held the eldest son designation. As with many families living near a dividing line of slavey beliefs, William and Clifton eventually found themselves surrounded by groups of opposing beliefs. As tensions grew these organizational beliefs created a fracture line in their relationship, and, in the early 1860's with war unfolding, older brother Clifton attached himself to the Union army, while younger brother William migrated south to attach himself to the Confederate army.

As the war raged on and armies marched themselves towards an impending battle the brothers unknowingly traversed a path of destiny. On April 2nd, 1865 the Union forces, commanded by heralded General Ulysses S. Grant, brought a full on assault on General Lee's Confederate forces. At the battle's end, two brothers lay gravely wounded on the battlefield, within closer distance than could have ever been crafted had this been written into the dramatic twist of a fictional theatrical performance.

Knowing through intel that there was a chance his brother was part of the defending Confederate forces, Clifton had his brother brought over and laid next to him. With life-giving blood draining from his shattered leg, William reached out to the hand of his brother, who lay unable to speak with a devastating wound to his lung. On May 14th both brothers were transferred to Armory Square Hospital in Washington DC.

A month after arriving, William succumbed to his wounds. Two months later his brother would pass away at home from his battle injuries. To add one more note of infamy to this story, one of the greatest poets in the history of our country, Walt Whitman, was providing support to the injured soldiers at Armory Square Hospital. The weight of the Prentiss brother tragedy led to the composition of the following story:

May 28-9. — I staid to-night a long time by the bedside of a new patient, a young Baltimorean, aged about 19 years, W. S. P., (2d Maryland, southern,) very feeble, right leg amputated, can't sleep hardly at all — has taken a great deal of morphine, which, as usual, is costing more than it comes to. Evidently very intelligent and well bred — very affectionate — held on to my hand, and put it by his face, not willing to let me leave. As I was lingering, soothing him in his pain, he says to me suddenly, "I hardly think you know who I am — I don't wish to impose upon you — I am a rebel soldier." I said I did not know that, but it made no difference. Visiting him daily for about two weeks after that, while he lived, (death had mark'd him, and he was quite alone) I loved him much, always kiss'd him, and he did me. In an adjoining ward I found his brother, an officer of rank, a Union soldier, a brave and religious man, (Col. Clifton K. Prentiss, sixth Maryland infantry, Sixth corps, wounded in one of the engagements at Petersburg, April 2 — linger'd, suffer'd much, died in Brooklyn, Aug. 20, '65.) It was in the same battle both were hit. One was a strong Unionist, the other Secesh; both fought on their respective sides, both badly wounded, and both brought together here after a separation of four years. Each died for his cause.

The story of the Prentiss brothers illustrates the impact the people and ideas around us can imprint on our life actions. If your overarching goal is to move in the direction of paternal involvement, then fatherhood groups are an essential step in staying the course. There are a number of groups you can connect with. I will refer a few to you but a simple google search can guide you down a number of valuable roads. In addition, getting a group together among your friends is also highly recommended. Here is a list of some good places to start in no particular order:

- https://citydadsgroup.com

- https://childrenstrustma.org/our-programs/fatherhood-initiative

Join a Fatherhood Group

- https://www.facebook.com/groups/dadsdaughters/

- https://www.facebook.com/groups/dadswithsons/

- https://www.facebook.com/fatheringtogether/

- https://www.facebook.com/groups/bnfsupport/

- https://www.instagram.com/explore/tags/fatherhood/

You will also be able to more than likely find a parenthood group in your local area. Do a google search and see what your city/state has for options. Thus, operation numero dos, join a fatherhood group, simple as that.

Paint By Numbers

Operation 3:

Ditch the God-Damn Phone

Paint By Numbers

I was 13 years old in the summer of 1990, and the debut single, "Vision of Love", from what is now music icon Mariah Carrey, dominated the charts all through that hot month of August. It had been two years since my life was impacted forever following a tragic plane crash that had taken the life of a friend's mother. I heard the crash, rather, I should say I felt the crash.

Here's what happened:

As the winter of 1988 approached, a meager New England Patriots team took their home field against the division rivals Miami Dolphins. The Patriots would finish 9-7 that year, and, before the dynasty we have become accustomed to had risen, that was considered a good year! I was sitting inside a nicely appointed, modernly designed home with someone whom I would have proclaimed my best friend in the whole world at the time.

With over 30 years of time between this moment and that fateful day, I am sure some of my memories are self-manifested. However, the generality of the day would have been like many Sundays spent with him. Sprawled out on the large sectional sofa, eating what was more than likely a sugar and saturated fat delicious treat. I mean shit, we were the Little Debbie generation baby! At that age, watching the game was a passive event, so I can't tell you if it was a commercial or the most amazing catch of the game that had happened. What I can tell you is that I felt a vibration through the house, the way you experience a large object falling off a bureau and resonating its impact waves throughout the 2x4's, plywood, and sheetrock encompassing the structure. More than something falling, it felt deeper, heavier.

What else I can tell you is that at that moment, the wiser, older individuals in the room, were sure it was more, and out the front door they went. You see, one thing kids are excellent at is spotting panic or concern in a parent's voice. As eleven-year-old boys, on a normal hum-drum day in November, we latched on to that concern in the manner in which Kelly Slater grabs that 20-foot whitecap and begs for it to take him where it may. Little did we know that at that moment, the ocean tide was pulling hard toward a rocky shore; but when you're in the wave, you're in the wave, and she's going to take you wherever she wants.

When I first set my eyes upon the scene, there were two immediate pictures that my brain processed. The initial was the site of our schoolmate, friend and neighbor running towards us more upset than my young life had ever witnessed. There were tears...lots of tears streaming down her young adolescent face. There were words. Garbled and panic words that were tough to follow, but it was clear she wanted help. I said nothing, just stood frozen and confused. Confused by the second site which was clearly a remote-controlled plane, whose operator was just learning how to navigate the controls, and sent it nose-down into the field.

I looked at her hysteria, and then my gaze floated back to the plane when a third image came into focus. It was her father, permeating with the same madness and running towards the downed, remote-controlled plane, pleading for the same help which my friend was requesting. And at that point, her garbled speech regained clarity, and, with the revelation of someone learning a new language, I understood all that I needed to understand. "My mom is in the plane"! My mind refocused, and through the wonders of our minds' eyes, I could now see the miscalculation in size and spatial recognition of what I was actually seeing. That was not a fucking remote-control plane.

Almost immediately, with sirens in the distance, the three of us were ushered back into my friend's home, and back onto that sectional couch with the Little Debbie wrappers now lying empty on the floor, a site which in any other situation would have been unlawful in this home. We sat in silence. Tears and sobs streamed down the face of our friend as she contemplated the likelihood of her mother's survival. Apparently, her mom was on a sightseeing flight doing a flyover of the house while the rest of the family waved from below. A picture-perfect moment had been turned into an unimaginable tragedy. After a few minutes, which had seemed like hours, her father walked into the house and ushered her out to utter the sentence she must have predicted. The remainder of the day has dissolved from my memory.

It is now almost 2 years since that fateful day, and my father and I are taking the short walk from our house to the crash site. The intent wasn't to visit the site, moreover it was likely an activity at the end of the summer to stem the boredom exhibited by an adolescent who has exhausted almost all of the sleepovers, pool parties and pick-up football games my parents could muster. The road we walked was indicative of a middle-class town with each home perched atop nicely manicured multi-acre lots. Aged lush trees created a canopy providing shade for most of the quarter mile straight away, leading to the one ninety-degree left bend in the road. At the end of the bend, the field to the right where the crash had occurred was now in the planning stages of a housing subdivision, with a temporary road already cleared through the brush and high grass.

The vision of the field was what prompted the discussion with my father. Up until that point it had been a fairly silent walk. We talked. There were perceptions and emotions that two years of adolescent development allowed me to more fittingly communicate, and he listened intently, offering reassurance and feedback where appropriate. The more we conversed, the slower our walk progressed, allowing time for silence and processing. That summer, I was able to process and accept what happened in that field. It was the availability of my father that brought about that clarity. I learned to accept the fragility of life and for the first time realized my own mortality.

Throughout my life, I had numerous interactions like this, gaining insight, support, and direction from my father; however there is something about this memory that stands out to me in reflecting on my own parenting. That August day, when my father and I stepped outside of the house and walked out of earshot of my mother, something happened....we were unreachable. At no point during the gentle saunter was my father's cell phone going to ring. It didn't exist; at least yet in our household. The entire walk was just he and I, uninterrupted and connected. I've had these walks and talks with my children, but in full unabashed honesty, there are times I forget to leave that damn phone home.

There are times that my focus, which should be on the excitement in my son's voice, is instead on the uttered homily reverberating from my phone speaker. In these moments I must reorientate myself and take that phone out of earshot. I have to consciously remove myself from its beckoning call, allowing myself to focus my attention where it belongs.

Now I know that this is not always possible, and yes, there are times that work must take precedence over whatever is going on at home. However, I will always have time to put my phone out of reach for a good portion of my night or weekend, to ensure I can provide that same focus of intention that my father provided me back in August of 1990, a year I needed him immensely, and thankfully, he was there. So for operation number three, put the damn phone away....please!

Why Batting Averages Are So Important

If I were to rank my favorite sports in order of preference it would probably go soccer, football, any type of one-on-one fighting (wrestling, MMA, etc), and then baseball. However, what has always intrigued me about baseball above all other sports, is how effectively it uses statistics to rank its players. Any Boston Red Sox fan worth their weight in gold could tell you that the .406 club, now termed the EMC club after corporate buyout, is in honor of the Hall of Famer Ted Williams, who, in 1941 batted .4057, placing him 17th on the all-time batting average list since baseball stats have been recorded. To put this in perspective, the closest to even touch this in the modern era was Tony Gwynn, who in 1994 batted .3938. No player since Ted Williams has batted over .400.

See how easy that is to quantify how exceptional Ted Williams was? Statistics in baseball can make things very clear. Now, with that being said, I know many of you are looking at this chapter and saying "Oh no, I didn't buy this book to revisit the C+ I received in Stats 101!" So here's my compromise. I think this is very important. Statistics, as evident from the excellence of my buddy Ted, are very relevant; however, they can be extremely boring. I promise to keep this section fairly short and to the point, while adding in some entertaining vignettes, if you promise not to skip on. It's important to me that you realize the extent of the crisis, and just like the .406 Club at Fenway, the stats will clearly paint that picture. Therefore, before we go on to Operation 4, let's have another reminder of why this topic we are discussing is so important.

Paint By Numbers

The Fatherless Generation provides a great synopsis of some very staggering statistics. Did you know that.......

- Over 60% of youth suicides occur in families without a father.

- Over 70% of high school dropouts – yup, fatherless homes.

- 80% of rapists with anger problems – you guessed it, no dad at home growing up.

- 90% of homeless runaways – yup, you're catching on.

In those stats, in that specific order, the rates are 5, 9, 14 and 32 times the national average respectively. If you have an involved father you are five times less likely to commit suicide. That one brings tears to my eyes. Time to Man Up! Ted Williams was an amazing hitter; our children need involved fathers; and I need you to give a shit about the stats.

Now research abounds in this area (despite the fact that many people who should be following the statistics are clearly not....more on them later), and we could look at so many areas: fatherhood on drug abuse, fatherhood on education, fatherhood on mental health, fatherhood on criminal behavior, fatherhood on incarceration, but like I said, I promised to keep this section short. In order to do that and still make my point I am going to focus on just a few: incarceration rates, education, and female sexual activity. The last of those I hold very close to my heart. My daughter and step daughters are all princesses and I am driven to ensure they realize how a man should treat them.

Prison is an amazing concept. On a recent late winter morning, while the local network anchor informed me of another above average temperature day (God bless global warming!!), I finished tying my double windsor knot (yes ladies and gentlemen, I can dress like my man Slick Rick......fresh to def!) and the news switched to the story of a young man. Barely out of high school, this boy experienced the heart wrenching feeling of watching his recent ex-girlfriend kissing another boy.

When we see an image, an amazing process occurs. Initially, our eyes process the amount of incoming light in various degrees. This incoming light then gets relayed from the retina through the part of the brain called the thalamus and into the primary visual cortex. This part of the brain consists of thickly packed cells, layered together. From there, the information is organized in the brain and processed as color, shape, movement and location. Of all these inputs, the contrast of the light that is processed appears to be the most significant in affecting what we "see". The beauty of the human mind can be seen in the horrific aftermath of the light that was processed through that young man's primary visual cortex.

Light turned to image. Image turned to emotion, which in this case was anger. Anger turned to action, which was to burn the home of the women who had just caused him such pain, and, in turn, send two men living in the apartment building to an early rendezvous with their maker. Now, months later, the light entering this young boy's eyes will be processed as a deep brown desk, situated on a raised platform in a purposeful attempt to elicit a presence of power. The light will also process a man or woman, situated behind that desk in a black robe as almost all judges have become accustomed to wearing. The sentencing will be the most difficult part as the trial was unnecessary following the young man's admission of guilt. Will it be twenty five years? The news reporter evaluates the various levels of sentencing in the same manner he had just informed his listeners that the Boston Celtics had just reeled off their fifth straight win. All in all it is just another sixty second piece which will be reported, filed away and forgotten about along with the hundreds of other convictions that occur and are reported on daily.

Tomorrow, after his sentencing, the light entering the young man's eyes will consist of metal bars, separating his tiny living space from the world. One week from now, the light entering the young man's eyes will be the same. Ten years from now, the light entering the man's eyes will still be unchanged. Twenty four years from now, the light now entering this older man's eyes, possibly through necessary glasses at this point, will again be unchanged. Is it deserved? I do believe so. Taking life must be punished. And then I begin to think about the young boy's father, who may or may not be present or even alive. And then I begin to think of my son and stepson, and the unfathomable concept that every dream, hope and aspiration I have for them could be rotting behind those metal bars for 25 years. I very well could be dead when they are finally set free.

An article on the Mentoring Project, an organization out of Portland, Oregon providing mentorship for fatherless children and adolescents, Relevant Magazine noted some staggering statistics. Over twenty seven million adolescents in 2009 were growing up without fathers and directly in line with that statistic was the 85% of incarcerated young men who grew up in fatherless homes.

How Did We End Up Here?

We have something in common. In the same fashion you are reading this book for a reason, I also wished to write this book for a reason. So before we go on with the Operations, I wanted to provide you with a bit more on my journey which led me to this final product.

Our common connection is a genuine love and care for the children that are in our lives in one form or another. Now here's the cliché part of the book. The next paragraph will be the most played out, overly stated verbiage the world has known. Just like lower back tattoos on middle aged women and overly enlarged holes in the ears of misunderstood youth, the next paragraph will feel just as cheesy. However, a cliché is a cliché for a reason, because we can all relate. We will refer to the next paragraph as the tramp stamp of the book.

On September 5th, 2006 my life changed in a way that I could have never imagined. On that day at 9:49 in the morning, I held my daughter in my arms for the first of which has proven to be countless embraces throughout her life. I watched as the doctors weighed her and saw the world as I hadn't seen it since my early childhood, with wonder, amazement, and joy. My ears processed her first cry, one of many I have heard in my life as a father, except this one was different. It was the validation that air had entered her lungs, eliminating one of the first parental fears. Then finally, as I caught my breath, I stood back and realized a fact that I continue to hold as truth.................she was perfect! Again, amazingly, on August 2nd, 2009, I repeated those actions in the exact same delivery room, at almost the exact same time and was left holding my son (who was extremely well endowed for a newborn....he was my boy after all!). There are few actions in life where the rush of emotion doesn't lessen after the initial experience. The birth of a child is one of the few, and as I stood looking at that beautiful boy, watching his clenched hands wave in the jerky, seemingly uncontrolled fashion, exploring unrestricted movement for the first time; I again realized a fact that I continue to hold as truth...................he was perfect!

Fifteen years from the birth of that first child at the time of this books publication and despite their perfection, both have on numerous occasions came within seconds of being returned.......... and I wouldn't have even asked for a refund. Kids have the ability to take you on those emotional roller-coasters that make the Superman ride at Six Flags seem like a lazy river float. Amazingly, out of love and understanding, we let the emotions fade away, come back down to reality, and press forward while providing them the love and stability that they need.

In the initial years of my children's lives; my now ex-wife and I provided them with the experiences common among many middle class American children. Family game nights, trips to the playground, youth activities, countless birthday parties and family vacations all become memories that are still ingrained in me. This is good, but only for me, because my children remember absolutely none of them. (My next book will be "How to waste a lot of fucking money on things your kids will never remember". It will be a New York Times best seller!)   Throughout this time I watched them change and grow. It's so easy to see the visible effects of children as they change. Relatives will come over after weeks without seeing the children and utter the same similar greeting: "Look how big you're getting", "You're getting so grown up"; you know them all. The hardening of the facial features, muscular and skeletal development, improved balance and dexterity are all easy identifiers of the change within the children. One-word utterances become two to three word sentences. "She's so smart", they'll say. Yup, she's a real Einstein, capable of asking for more cake by uttering the sounds, "moah peeeze". Call Harvard now, we got ourselves a winner! Point being, the changes are obvious, and easily identifiable through small samples of behavior.

What's not so obvious, however, are the incredible changes that occur inside us as men. The building blocks of human behavior are primarily shaped as a child. Your core personality is often solidified very early in life. However, for many men, the initial cry of your child as it takes its first breath of air, must have a powerful effect on the physiological state. Neurochemistry that was running on autopilot for years seems to experience a shift.

I liken the neurological change that happened to me to the process we see in a small seed of grass. The seed in itself sits idle, looking almost dead and lifeless in its resting state. (And if we are referring to my front lawn, it would stay that way.....forever!) One rainy day, the motionless seed, now bathed in the life-giving breath of water, begins to drink. It is the water resting on its surface that spurs it into action in the same fashion that the sound of the first whale of my child wrapped itself around some dormant neurons in my brain, early childhood ones that had lay lifeless for years, and gently whispered "drink". We cannot see the seed begin to drink, and I can imagine the quiet, repetitive whispers continuing to slowly provoke the neurons into action.

Eventually, through constant prodding, spurred on by the laughs, cries, shared moments and the irreplaceable bond of a father and a child, the faintest electrical spark ignites in the previously dormant neuron. It had slowly drunk and drunk and drunk, and now it is alive again. This process will continue, gradually and almost unnoticeably, the way grass grows in my neighbor's yard, and, before you know it a new lawn is present. A new man is present.

Look at your friends, acquaintances, enemies. Look at any of them and every one of us can identify the complete douchebag. The John Bluto Blutarsky played by John Belushi in the now famous movie Animal House. We all know one or two of those in our social network. I had many of these friends growing up; some may actually say that I WAS one of these friends, but I would deny that fervently. Well ok, there was this one period of time that falls directly into the bucket of least proud moments. I use the plural form of the word moment in that sentence because it became a thing I did; and it is against all of my best judgement that I will share this story with you.

The year was around 2004. I can't say for sure exactly, but I like to think that this time period occurred before I hit my 30's, so for that sake we will go with 2004. Furthermore, 2004 was an amazing year for a New England sports fan. The Patriots won their second Super Bowl title in three years and the Boston Red Sox ended a historic World Series drought. As an avid sports fan surrounded by other avid sports fans, there seemed always to be a party somewhere, watching one of our teams compete on a very high level. In addition, this was also the age where our friends began to start buying their own homes, making house warming parties a common occurrence. It was here, at one of these housewarming parties, that my story begins.

I recall the moment almost as clearly as I recalled to you the birth of my children, minus the complete rebirth of my soul that I earlier discussed. It was a warm mid-summer's day. As with most cookouts, the guests were invited to arrive around 2pm, but me, in what has become typical behavior, arrived later than most. As a result of my perpetual tardiness, the smells of burning charcoal and sounds of rambunctious twenty-something's was ever present as I made my way through the white gate and into the backyard. A few games of horseshoes, a number of drinks and a couple of burgers later, mother nature began to call, so I made my way into my friends new home. The house was beautiful! A large colonial with vaulted ceilings in the living area, an inviting kitchen and welcoming sitting area in front of a well-appointed fireplace. Having been involved in real-estate for some time at this point, I had developed a true appreciation for this kind of thing.

Strolling over to the downstairs bathroom I grabbed the handle and was met with a resounding "one-minute" from the current occupant. One minute became two, and two became three, so before it could become four, I made my way upstairs to the other bathroom. The door was ajar, and, as I approached the sense of relief that I would soon be able to relieve the pressure in my stomach from all the food and drink felt great. Then it happened. I can't tell you why, because I honestly don't know. Maybe it was the practical joker that has always lived inside me, or the quiet serenity that the space held amidst the bustle and noise of the downstairs and the outside yard; but in that moment I looked at the toilet and smirked.

Strolling over to the toilet, I lifted off the back cover, quietly enough so nobody would hear. Of course they wouldn't hear- nobody was upstairs and the party noise was enough to drown out most sounds. I stood myself up on the now closed toilet seat and performed the act most commonly referred to as the "Upper-

Decker". Trying my hardest to hold in my laughter, I carefully replaced the top of the toilet bowl, went downstairs, and continued on with the party like nothing had ever happened. That was the birth of "The Phantom Upper-Decker"! At least that is what I termed myself as nobody ever knew about my exploits but me.

The next day, when that poor unsuspecting friend couldn't figure out why dirty water permeated his toilet each time he flushed, the text messages began to fly. They were hilarious! Apparently there were a lot of jokesters in our group, and many worse than me because a bunch of people were getting accused, and I skated by unnoticed. That began my reign of terror. I made it a point to strike as many of our friends as possible during these housewarming parties, and I had many victims until finally one day, I struck in a moment where there wasn't a party, and the gig was up! The phantom "Upper-Decker" was caught, never to strike again.

Now I tell that story for two reasons. Primarily, it is absolutely hysterical that I made up a name for myself that only I knew, and the random nature of how the prank began. Most importantly, I tell the story because in the typical fashion of John Bluto Blutarsky, those actions should clearly disqualify me from ever being allowed to rear anything.....especially a child. However, as with many other men like me, those neurological changes that spawn from the sounds of our children in the early years have made me the man I am today. Not that I don't still joke around and pull pranks, because I do, but now, with everything I do, and every move I make, I think to myself, "What would my children think and what do I want them to learn." That is how I ended up here, writing this book under the realization that our children need good fathers.

How Did We End Up Here

For those of you wondering, don't worry, I paid the price of the Phantom Upper Decker exploits with countless pranks and stunts played on me by my friends. Tell you what, I deserved every one of them!

Paint By Numbers

Operation 4:

Meet Them Where They Are!

Paint By Numbers

My children walk around my damn house, blinded to the world around them, and perform these rhythmic hand motions that remind me of the hearing impaired box in the corner of the television during the Governor's most recent press update. Intuitively, I look around, searching intently for the receiver of these mysterious communication forms. When that fails, my feeble mind then jumps directly to a thorough examination of their ear canals in search of what is surely an embedded air-pod. Still nothing. Now, my parental fear kicks in full force, as it must be an epileptic seizure.

Acting with the swiftness of a well-trained first responder, I immediately get them to the ground and positioned on their side, directing the other members of the home to clear away surrounding furniture to avoid injury during the inevitable seizure. It's not until the confused eyes of the child stare up at me and clearly verbalize his or her displeasure in my actions that I realize I may have overreacted. "What's going on with your hands?" I proclaim! "It's a tik-tok, Dad!", my child would ferociously declare. Ahhhh, of course it is. Well fuck you tik-tok and your ridiculous extremity animations!

It's tough man, it's real tough. In the depth of my heart, probably like many of my fellow fatherly figures out there, I find a majority of the handheld device fads of our children's generation to be completely ridiculous, but they don't. Oh no, not at all. You see, within the cosmos of an adolescent brain, there exists not a vast expanse of possibilities, worlds, options and systems. In actuality, if you take the opening to Tyson deGrasse's famous interstellar show and play it in reverse, that is the myopic view of our little ones. The end of that scene I just described, the camera would break through Earth's atmosphere, making a meteoric fall back through the clouds, between the skyscrapers of city life, down on to the streets and into the hands of a 13 year old girl, where would lie, an iPhone 11s-double-d (I made that model up, but if they ever come out with it I want one!). With fingers tapping away with the rapid flutter of a hummingbird, the child makes her communications to the world, and in that, the scene ends.

Fuck you cellular device, for stealing the last days of enjoying life with my adolescent child, before she reverts to that 8 year period of complete surety that we are of no use to them.

Here we are, stuck with these robotic children whom we are trying to guide, yet who are parma-gripped to these Chinese tracking devices masquerading as communication mechanisms. What the shit! Men, we only have one option here, one chance to break through the military grade concrete walls that are slowly being erected day by day. We've got to download that fucking app. Now for our millennials, especially those of you born towards the latter part of that generational gap, you're probably fine with this. In reality, you're probably competing with your children for social status superiority.

For the remainder of us, we need to pursue the guidance of these damn millennials and get on board because they are onto something. No, don't misrepresent my words here. All this shit is completely idiotic and a waste of time for 99% of its use. However, seeing our children are also completely idiotic in many ways, what better way to connect with them.

For me, I started with snapchat. My morning routine consisted of the usual trek to school. Recently risen children, sitting in quiet somnolence. With my son, I was cool with that daily start. Following the caravan of minivans and SUVs embarking on the head jerking stop-and-go parade of student drop off at the middle school, we would say goodbye to his sister and head to our favorite breakfast spot before his school day began an hour later. With him, at those hundreds of diner meals, we made countless memories and had some great connection time. However, with my daughter, all I had was that fleeting 20 minute car ride to the school.It was here I noticed her snapchat pattern.

"Why are you taking pictures of half of your face"? I would inquire. Inevitably, with the gaze of someone who was just asked why breathing is important, my daughter would simply reply with her stone faced, half-woke look, return to her pressing task of snapping out of frame images and ignore my ridiculous question. As a father I was left with two options. I could fight this routine on a daily basis, which, to be honest had no more detrimental effect than the lack of communication it was providing for the two of us; or, I could take the red pill instead of the blue pill and join in.

So option two it was, and that day at work, I downloaded every social media app she was using, and then, with the recollection of the morning commute I had just experienced, I went to the first one on my mind and opened snapchat. At this moment I likened myself to a teenage Jenifer Connelly, trudging obstinately through the labyrinth of emoji buttons and options presented on the screen before me. Eventually, after about 30 minutes of clueless exploration, I had successfully sent a friend request to my daughter. To my surprise, despite the incriminating action of accepting the request in the middle of school, clearly exposing her lack of adherence to the "no phones in class" rule, we were "friends". Thus began my streak with my daughter of blurry shots of half of my face. The good half of course!

The aftereffect of this action, along with my simultaneous request for friendship in her other social media apps, had a multitude of positive fruitions. Most consequential was the increase in verbal interactions whenever I would send her a digital outreach. I would send the most ridiculous, ostentatious content to her, strictly for the reaction and engagement. To further this, I also realized that allowing her to have a bit more leniency with what would be acceptable communication also increased her communications with me through these new forms.

Ok, so let me sum that up, Short story is that if we are texting back and forth I may let a "dad, you're being a douche" comment go by with less repercussions than if that was said to my face. My rationale for that was it allowed the conversation of how people can "hide" behind the screen and say and do things they would never do to someone's face. These conversations became teaching moments that our social media interactions precipitated.

In addition to our increased interactions that were spurred on by our newfound digital relationship, this dynamic also allowed us the framework to create a digital media contract. This contract was written jointly by the two of us and set limits for how to behave and interact on all of the digital content that adolescents use to communicate. We both signed the contract and placed some guidelines and "punishments" around breaking the contract. Some examples of our rules are listed below:

- There is absolutely no fighting over text messages or other social media platforms. If you are upset, you will let the person know that you want to discuss the problem face to face.

(This rule was excellent for also teaching kids how to handle issues with friends that occur over this platform)

- There is no sending pictures of anything that you would not want the world to see if it was on the evening news. (We call this one "passing the channel 10 test")

- There is absolutely no talking bad about someone else when on a text chain with a friend. (Screenshots can be a social killer!)

There were others but those are just some ideas that you can use to create your own social media contract. We are all artists, and each one of our children will have different needs that we will have to mold our contract to fit.

The act of meeting my child in his or her current social and emotional space paid far greater dividends than the path of ridicule and harassment that so readily flowed to the tip of my tongue upon gazing down on them completely engrossed in their digital world. There are many ways, that this act can increase your connectedness with the young ones in your life.

For example, my son absolutely loves to draw. I, on the other hand, have yet to find the act of drawing or painting very relaxing. I believe my innate nature to want to get to the finale of my work makes the process of drawing and painting a bit painstaking for me.[4] Regardless, my son's love of art promoted the act of us drawing together. We will sometimes play a

---

[4]Even with this book there were moments where I contemplated sitting in front of my computer for 72 hours straight just to get the damn thing done! If you study the prose closely you may find the section of the book where that attempt failed miserably.

game where we sit across from each other, set a timer, and pass a drawing back and forth. We each get a minute or two to add to the drawing, and, then, after a predetermined amount of time, we have a combined work.

This exercise then spurs great conversation where he discusses what he was trying to do, and I discuss what I was trying to do. Weaved into the conversation are the life lessons of compromise, flexibility, and appreciation for another view-point. The act is fun for him and hits some of my parental teaching goals all at once by simply meeting him where he is at and getting him into an enjoyable receptive state.

As I culminate this section, I want you to ruminate on the countless times we ask our children to meet us where we are. Count the number of times they watch a show, engage in an activity or perform a chore or act because it is what we need or like. Shit, when you spend some time pondering it, we ask our kids to meet us where we are all the damn time. Carve out some time in your schedule as referenced in Operation 1 to meet them where they are and you will surely reap the benefits.

Paint By Numbers

Operation 5:

Acknowledge We Are All Fuckups.

Have you ever really visualized the commonplace saying of "falling on your sword"? The adage, so commonly referred to, holds its roots in both ancient Roman and Japanese culture. The most notable tale of this act takes place with Brutus. Marcus Junius Brutus was a Roman senator around the time of Julius Ceasar and was one of the key players involved in the assassination plot on their infamous leader.

At a later point in his life, following a major military defeat, the story goes that Brutus requested the assistance of a friend with his suicide by sword. When his friend failed to comply, Brutus fell to the ground, thrusting his weight onto the tip of his sword and into his abdomen, thus killing him. For clarity, the remaining words in this chapter will not advocate this method of punishment should we fuck up as parents. Just want to be really, really clear here.

One of the common misconceptions we all have when examining individuals, whom we view as successful in their respective fields, is the lens of constant success we tend to view them through. The casual drive-by of our favorite house in a well-manicured, sprawling acreage section of town, often elicits romantic images of the blissful existence behind the walls. The swaggering gate of Davonte Adams as he crossed the goal-line for the league-leading 18th time in 2020 imprints upon us an image of universal success. In this same fashion, the many blog posts, meetings and seminars I have heard throughout the years on the topic of parenting and fatherhood, often result in that same gaze of wonderment at the perfection of the speaker. That guy must be the best fucking dad ever! Well, I call bullshit! We all are fuck-ups, and the best thing about our mistakes is the ability to show humility and accept error in front of those we are trying to mold so, thus, fall on our proverbial sword. I believe that this operation may be the most critical of the eight; the most influential and beneficial in developing a relationship of trust and love with the children in our lives that we are trying to guide, mold and influence.

"Say you're sorry"! We proclaim that statement to our children, and the kids we are teaching, molding and guiding with the regularity of a washed-up Samuel L Jackson asking me what I have in my wallet. Back off Sam, back off. I got cash money in my wallet, mother fucker, better question is what's in your wallet? Celebritynetworth.com has your net worth at $250,000,000. Let's talk about what's in your wallet and how I can get my hands on some of that. Anyway, I do love me some SLJ. His portrayal of Jules Winfield in that Quentin Tarantino classic was a top ten role of all time and in line with our current concept SLJ does say he is sorry in his famous sermon to the three panicked kids he wittily interrogates in their apartment. Although, "I'm sorry, did I break your concentration" after firing a warning shot into the couch next to one of the petrified boys may not be the honest apology we are looking for here.

In reflecting on our requests for an authentic atonement from our children, it is clear that we ask this of them with regularity. Any time our young children cause harm to another child or to us as parents, we force out of them these two magic words "I'm Sorry". How then, can we best display the importance of that apology? We absolutely must model the behavior with sincerity and towards an end goal of understanding. You see, apologies are a tricky thing, and I think they need to come in a few forms to truly produce the results of which we are looking. I think it's time for a story.

I have a temper. Ever since I was a young child my biggest issue was losing control of my emotions and behaving in a way that is embarrassing, which causes me a lot of shame and guilt and goes against everything I believe is the way in which I want to model conflict management. As I have gotten older, my ability to utilize strategies to keep my emotions under control has gotten better and better. However, every once in a while I fail; and I despise failing! Often people comment on how calm and controlled I am in situations of stress and tension. I can say here, that is not a natural thing for me. It has come as a direct result of me hating the person I am when I let those shackles come off.

The year is 2011 and my first marriage is failing. A tension between my now ex-wife and I permeates most conversations, and, for some reason, we are arguing. I don't recall the issue, but I recall the scene with extremely vivid detail. Our cedar shingled 1,100sq/ft gambrell home sat nestled on a multi-acre parcel in a small valley, surrounded by a few neighbors and mainly woods, streams, and a small pond. It was a quiet wooded area on a road, that witnessed little traffic, just about five miles from the center of our town. The house was small and cozy with a spiral staircase leading up to a master bedroom. The master bedroom had cathedral ceilings, bamboo wood floors and dual French doors which opened out to a private deck overlooking the backyard that was framed by a fairly dense wooded forest.

On summer nights you could sit out and be amazed by the clarity in the night sky which lacked any major light pollution and the sounds of nature resonated throughout the woods. On this night the doors and windows were closed as we jockeyed for verbal position in another frustrating exchange. Eventually, my emotions began to rise, and I could feel the heat in my face, intention of my gaze, and loss of verbal control that I strived so hard to maintain. At that exact moment, seeing my failing control and with the precision aim of a marksman, my ex-wife released the quiver on her verbal arrow sure it would hit its target. The strike of the arrow dislodged the cork holding my endorphins at bay, and with that blow, the man I hate emerged.

My voice escalated, my words became hurtful, and the cordless phone I was holding in my hand took flight. Having disassociated from my surroundings at this point, I paid no attention to the fact that the phone now flew directly towards one of our bedroom windows, striking it perfectly and sending it into shattered pieces on the floor. In unfortunate synchrony with that event, my daughter slowly crept her way up the spiral staircase to see what the argument was about. She crested the visual barrier of the room at the exact moment the phone struck the window, sending shock and fear deep into her body. My ex-wife scooped her up, escorted her downstairs and began consoling her. To this day, my daughter remembers that event as clearly as I do. That shame burns deep in me a decade later.

How in the name of God do we expect a few iterated words, "I'm Sorry", to fix the image and impact of that event on our children? The same two words that we will mandate our child say if he or she sneaks an extra treat after dinner or grabs a toy from a friend or sibling. Are these two things really so aligned in nature that the response for each should also be identical. Obviously not, so to initiate our atonement, yes we must start with the "I'm Sorry". As soon as we regain focus and control a measured and sincere apology to those that were witness to our transgression needs to happen. At that moment do not expect or accept a response of acquiescence. The goal of this is not to free yourself of the responsibility, rather to let those around you know that you accept responsibility and have recognized you're wrong. That action will serve to dissipate the existing tension.

The follow up to this, is even more important, for its the discussion and reliving of the event, that will be the true healer for all involved. Once the emotions have cleared, set a time to revisit the incident with the children and anyone else involved, and don't let too much time pass. If the event occurs early in the day have an evening sit down. If later in the day, schedule a time for the next day to discuss the incident. In this setting the opportunity is now created for you to express how you felt in the moment, how you reacted, and how you should have reacted. Give the children their opportunity to talk about how they felt and provide you with feedback on your behavior. I will even allow my 11 year old to tell me I was being a douche! Because I probably was!

The final step to this is restating your apology and providing them a plan for how you will try to do better next time. The modeling of a plan for improvement will help them create strategies for themselves and take accountability when they experience one of the many behavioral gaffes they are sure to engage in. You then in turn must commit yourself to improving. Apologies work if we follow through on our promise of taking active steps, giving credibility to the promise of a better you the next time around.

One of the most difficult characteristics to impart on our children is accountability. They are taught, through so many different channels, the art of blaming others and experience how much easier it is as a way forward. The art of modeling a successful two-staged apology will assist in the connectivity between you and the children. If dad or coach or mentor can err and own up to it, then I can too. The next time, therefore, that you force another "I'm Sorry" out of the children in your life, reflect on your own modeled penance, and if you're leading from the front, or ordering from the rear.

<u>*Paint By Numbers*</u>

Operation 6:

Say and Show Love

Paint By Numbers

What makes love songs so popular? Ok, let's not go tough guy here and pretend like that sappy shit sucks, and you would never listen to it unless you were 100% sure it was going to lead to some sweet ass sexy-time as a result. Now, granted, that's usually my play as well. Additionally, I spent a good number of hours of my life rocking out to a little Boys 2 Men - "I'll Make Love To You" back in the wonderful year of 1994....and probably in 2021, too.

Look back at the Billboard top 100 songs every year and in the top 20 will always be a steady 20-25% in the love songs genre. You know why? Because inevitably we all want to be loved it is 100% human nature to wish for connectedness, acceptance, and love from the ones around us. Love is the metaphysical braiding that intertwines our bodily relation to one another, and the verbal and tangible proclamations of love serve to fortify the strands within those braids. Hug your kids and tell them you love them....got it?

We all have different love languages. The over 13 million copies of Dr. Chapman's "*The 5 Love Languages*" is a clear testament to both the human appetite for and intricacy of that four letter word. Therapists make a living on it. Lawyers exploit millions from it. Producers depict the complexity of it, and human nature prospects invariably for it. With children, the complexities of love can be extremely overwhelming, and their understanding of our love for them is often concealed by the perfunctory operations of our daily lives. The preparation of daily meals, time ,and effort spent on their recurring needs, countless duber trips (that's daddy-uber for you slower folks), and endless other actions that are activated unconsciously by our innate love for them do not naturally catalogue themselves as practices of love in the mind of a child. They are too complex, too vague, and require a far greater understanding and empathic proficiency for a young mind to accurately grasp. Therefore, it is up to us to simplify this love language, no matter how uncomfortable or out of character it may be for some of us.

Now, Dr. Chapman would probably disagree with me here and state that we need to find our child's love language and embrace it. However, I believe that no matter how we or they innately profess our love, it is imperative that we display that to children both verbally and physically during their younger years.

Rewinding back to the first chapter of this book, I told a story of my graduation from military basic training. In that recount, the imagery of my father verbalizing his pride in me was so ingrained in me that it will forever be one of the most memorable moments of my life. The reason for this lies in the scarcity with which my father would express these feelings and emotions towards his children. Now my sister and I never doubted that our father loved us, but we also knew it was rare for him to verbalize these feelings or display them with actions of affection like a hug or a kiss. That was just not his love language. What developed from that pattern was an oblivion to what my father felt about pretty much anything.

To this day, when it comes time to buy him gifts for his birthday or do something fun with him, my sister and I remain baffled as to what the fuck he would actually want or enjoy. Now, that doesn't mean that my father fails to enjoy things; to the contrary he almost always looks content and happy. What that means is that his happiness sitting on the couch, looks like his happiness when he first held his granddaughter. I'm saying, it is some Jedi mind control shit the way his emotions maintain such a level ground. While that attribute is one which I aspire to in many situations, it also impaired my capacity as a child to readily gauge his love for me. I could have used a few more "I love you"'s in those adolescent years, and thus I look to impart them now on the children in my life.

The act of showing and saying love may come naturally to some of you; but, to others, like my father, it may be a more forced activity. To hit this mark I am going to offer some suggestions.

One of the first methods I would recommend brings us back to Operation #1, get it on the calendar. The cyclone of life's necessities effortlessly obscures the love and commitment we strive to provide our cherished inner circle. We blink, and the day has ended, without an "I love you", without a show of gratitude or an acknowledgement of achievement. With none of this given, the day is done. This is why a calendar reminder to show love is so important. Get it on the calendar and consistently show your love. This act will not always result in an immediate message to a child or loved one. It will fortunately keep the concept on the forefront of your mind and help turn the behavior into a habit!

In an effort to also embrace my children where they are in their development, I try to make my communications fit into their lifestyle. As a result of having a split family, my children have the unfortunate reality of getting a phone call from whichever parent they are not currently with on that given day, checking in on them and seeing how their day is going: an important activity, and yet an aggravating burden for the teenagers who have minimal interest in this daily dialogue. Subsequently, I have resorted to sending text messages of love on a daily basis.

Somedays, I get a reply; somedays, radio silence. Regardless, through the beauty of iPhone technology,

Say And Show Love

I can see that my message was read and received. Mission accomplished. This has also had the added benefit of further increasing the quality of conversations when I do delve into the antiquated methodology of an actual telephone conversation. Send a text and send a reminder of love to the children in our lives. If it's random, unexpected and unsolicited it can have an impactful effect.

While I have advocated the importance of unpredictable declarations of affection, there are some life circumstances that unquestionably require us to say and show love. Conflict, Comfort, and Completion are my 3-C's for this concept. In parenthood there exists dispute, and when that conflict arises, and eventually subsides, it must be displaced by a consistent display of love. Furthermore, there are clear moments where our children require comfort, and in those settings the transparent verbalization of our love is essential. Lastly, the children in our lives are often completing tasks, some with minimal effort and some following laborious effort. In those latter moments, upon completion and regardless of outcome, our expression of love will serve as an honest validation of their effort! Make note of these 3-C's and work to implement them into your daily operation.

Paint By Numbers

Operation 7:

Control What You Can - Fuck the Rest

Paint By Numbers

It was 2pm, on what was another completed day at the school I had been working for quite some time. The hallway chatter among teachers had progressed to the inappropriate nature it always morphed into the minute the last student was loaded onto their bus home. "See you later, you little mother fuckers", we would mumble with a smiling wave as their faces peered through the rectangular clouded glass of the bus windows.

Now, before you get all righteous on me, let me defend our cathartic verbal releases. I worked as a school psychologist at a behavioral school full of students that had pissed off their home school administration to such an extent that they pretty much said, "get the fuck out"....and we in turn said, "get the fuck in"! With that context, know that on some days, no matter how much you wanted the best for these kids, you also wanted to strangle them after hour number 7. Furthermore, our staff was devoting 40 hours a week, of our lives, to the betterment of these kids, which in turn afforded us a free pass on those comments. I can call them motherfuckers because I endured the suffering of their torment, verbal and physical abuse, while still working on their behalf on a daily basis. However, if out in public with one of them ,and some stranger calls them a motherfucker, then I invoke my right to smash that son of a bitch. They haven't earned that right!

With that context cleared up, we can return to the end of day ritual I was depicting. As the students left, our staff would convene together in a small 10x20 conference room and debrief the day. Staff members would habitually adorn their ritualistic position around the oval wooden table, while a welcomed comment regarding the astounding incident of the day would unleash the barrage of verbal assault towards some unpresent child who had simply pushed them to their limit that day.

As the chatter died down and laughter settled, the conversation would eventually take on its intended purpose. In our line of work there was always a young child or adolescent who was struggling. In our line of work it often correlated to events going on in their home life. In our line of work there wasn't a fucking thing you could do about it.

For an entire work week, every week, we would toil away to improve the lives of the students with whom we worked. Like clockwork....literally, like clockwork, at 2pm daily we knew that student was about to get thrown back into the life that manifested a majority of their difficulties. Let me just say this. When you spend countless years in school, find a passion, implement the work necessary to exact change, and then a large percentage of your efforts are erased daily at 2pm; that pill cuts going down! With those cuts builds resilience and perspective that served me extremely well going forward as a parent, coach, and mentor. It is imperative to learn to say, "Fuck it" to the things that are out of your control. Those items cannot deter you from your effort nor deter your focus on a daily basis.

Releasing focus on the things outside of our control is a towering objective as a parent. It's why helicopter parenting became a thing; and while certainly not a proponent of this procreative approach, I relate to it conceptually. The yearning inside each of us to clear life's trail of brush, bramble and roots before allowing our children to pioneer its wilderness is rooted in our nature. In the early years we are further rewarded for this behavior.

Removing sharp objects, ensuring cribs are secure and gates are locked, delicately placing just the right amount of mashed nutrition into our children's mouths; each of these replicated actions serve to reinforce on a daily basis the importance of environmental control on our child's existence and success. Eventually, and with growing abandonment, the natural development of those children makes such securities implausible. Shit, the last thing we want to be is on the "bad parent" list because our child was hurt as a result of our failure to control these environments. The result is a societal pressure to ensure safety, and a locus of control expectation outside of anyone's feasible reach.

As a parent, mentor, coach or influential adult on a child, there will be a locus of control net. That net, based on your role and situation will always have varying size and compactness. A soccer net is magnificent at absorbing the energy from another one of Mohamed Salah's magnificent strikes; however, if our boy Mohamed tries to use that as his mosquito netting, he's fucked! With children and adolescents, this net is an altering substance.

The holes between its mesh grow with every year, so, in turn, we must adapt and accept the weakening control and safety we can provide. For me, I love that growth process; watching the adventure and capability our children discover through its process. I enjoy watching the net stretch, and elicit my subtle controls over it by predicting its expanse, and making small preemptive slits in certain areas for energy and growth to flow through.

Releasing control allows our children to experience jurisdiction over their decisions. Our role at these intersections is to provide some framework for the new experiences. The two issues that present for us in these situations are usually the interest of the child and our own comfort with shrinking that ever precious circle of control. For all of us this decision will almost never be identical to our peers. However, we often size up the soundness of our decision in relation to those peers. How the hell then do we put some constructs around these countless situations, variables, and decisions? I have one easy solution that I regularly use. It's called the 6 o'clock news test!

Imagine that something happened to your child, or a kid you're coaching. Don't go too dark on this one, fucked up shit can happen, it's part of life. In this scenario, imagine an injury or accident that someone could argue as preventable. If the local news was to show up with a camera and a microphone and ask you what happened. In your honest account, how would it sound?

Let me provide you with an example. There is a Dunkin Donuts about a mile from my house. The road leading to it is a fairly main road with a speed limit of about 45 miles per hour. At a certain age, each of my children have asked the question, "Dad, can I walk to Dunkin?", a simple question that leads us into the incalculable variables of potential disaster. What if someone tries to grab them or hurt them? What if a car hits them? On and on down the rabbit hole of "what if's." Solution: lights, camera, action, ...the 6 pm news test is on. "Mr. LaFauci", says the over-hairsprayed, makeup'd reporter. "What were you thinking letting your child make that dangerous walk"?

What's your response? If it starts with "Well, I was in a rush...." or "I didn't really think anything could happen?", then you probably made a poor decision. If your honest response is something to the effect of "Well, I went through my expectation with them, walk facing traffic, stay on the grass so you are far enough off the shoulder, have my number up in your phone so in an emergency you just need to hit send, text me when you get there and when you're on your way back.....etc, etc.". If those actions were what you would tell that news anchor, and it makes sense; then the net can probably be safely widened. Control the items you can to ensure good safety and guidance for them, and then you have to say, "I've controlled what I can.........Fuck the rest!".

This is the hardest part. As a parent it can consume our thoughts and manifest a cancer of self-doubt. As a coach, teacher, or mentor, it can deflate our sense of impact and value, making our full effort laborious at times. Components outside of our control can ironically control us to a much greater extent than we often recognize. Learning how to let them go is a billion-dollar industry in self-help and therapeutic expenses.

What does saying "fuck the rest" mean? It means staying purposeful and intentioned with our efforts despite the multitude of ways the world can derail our applications. It means full ownership of ourselves in charting our course forward, regardless of what others may do, say, or think. It means believing in the outcome and benefits of your actions and teachings, unconcerned with the prevailing beliefs of the time. It is the sole reason I created these operations, first for myself and now to share with you.

My operations allowed me to put focus and intention on the staggering undertaking of leading young minds in today's absolute bats in the belfry world we live in. In these operations I create focus, purpose, and direction. I believe wholeheartedly they will produce positive outcomes. How do I handle the billions of distractions, disturbances, and derailments that occur? In the words of one of my favorite songs, and Liverpool FC anthem *You'll Never Walk Alone*:

When you walk through a storm
Hold your head up high

Control What You Can - Fuck The Rest

And don't be afraid of the dark

At the end of a storm
There's a golden sky
And the sweet silver song of a lark

Walk on through the wind
Walk on through the rain
Though your dreams be tossed and blown

Walk on, walk on
With hope in your heart
And you'll never walk alone

You'll never walk alone

Walk on, walk on
With hope in your heart
And you'll never walk alone

You'll never walk alone

I set my course. I walk on. I say fuck the rest.

Paint By Numbers

Operation 8:

Give This Book to Someone.

Paint By Numbers

Yes, I know, how philanthropic of me to encourage a passing along of this book instead of just persuading another to buy the book and aid me on my way to a 1984 Porsche 911 with that massive black whale tail! Damn, that is some dope shit right there! With a 0-60 time of 5.3 seconds and a top speed of just under 150 mph, she is far from the pack leader against the muscle and technology of today. However, she is a classic icon with the curved body lines as discernible as the Nike swoosh.

Throughout time, the ability to create something new, exciting and flashy continues to come and go on a daily basis. Few however, have mastered the beauty of developing something whose function and beauty transcend time, fashion and technology. Well done Porsche, and despite my desire to obtain your purchase through this literary masterpiece, I forego my earthly possession for the opportunity to make a dent in the role of fatherhood on our children and paint my own timeless silhouette on our society. Therefore, as you come towards the conclusion of this book, and you read or listen to the final words inked on the pages, remember to hand this book off to the next reader, or hit "share" on the audiobook file, before sending it into the deep abyss of metabyte heaven.

A Story About My Stepdaughter

As this book comes to a close, I am ending with a story that looks closely at the impact and change social media has had on us as parents. Although it is in our face daily, its effects can be blurred by its regular immersion.

Just one generation ago, our children had minimal access to material and information, and as a result parents were able to monitor fairly well, their information stream. I can remember all too well as a kid growing up in the early 1990's how getting my hands on the latest issue of Playboy or Hustler was like finding a $100 bill between the couch cushions. Winner-winner chicken dinner! Social interactions were completely different. Aside from the random prank phone call, if you wanted to bully someone, you had to look them in the eye, square up with them and do it to their face. What then does this all mean for these kids as they grow up under the new rules of adolescence? We have no idea. The one thing we do know is that they will have had more exposure to material and situations that are far above their maturity level, and far more socially complex than any other children in the history of mankind. With that in mind, it is unequivocal that the need for a strong paternal figure in their life is more necessary than at any other point in history.

Let's look at just one example of this dynamic in play. The date is all too familiar to most of us for reasons we wish had never manifested such a branding, September 11th, 2001. On that day, children sat in their classrooms, listening intently (or distantly) to their teacher. Or some, quite older in age, stared across the room, hoping to make some form of eye contact with their soon to be boyfriend or girlfriend, wishing to share for one moment a smile that

113

inevitably, in the life of a teenager, would elicit physiological responses strong enough to be imprinted in their mind for the remainder of the day. Around the dinner table, when the inevitably repeated parental question "How was your day today?" was posed. It would be the first image to pass through their minds, yet the last to be uttered out for fear of embarrassment. More than likely the response of "Nothing!" is what we would hear before they would dive back into the mashed potatoes in an effort to avoid further questioning.

On that day, one classroom's experience was quite unique. President George Bush sat reading a childhood classic to a group of children who now have a quite different memory of that exciting day than was originally intended when the multitude of Presidential advisors had planned this visit. We all know the video images. The utter look of horror and racing thoughts were now clearly visible on a President's face, who had most certainly lost track of the story at hand and was deciding what his next move should be. Ironically, even for that classroom of children, kindergarteners through high school students across the country were for the most part oblivious to the actions of that day as they unfolded.

My 27 year old (at the time of the publishing of this book) stepdaughter, whose birthday actually falls on September 11th, can recall the event as if it was yesterday's news. The one detail that stands out apart from the actual events was the method in which kids were notified.

That day, most schools hid this information from their students, allowing the day to go on, avoiding panic, and sending letters home informing parents that they should be the ones to inform their children. Schools that did inform their students did so in a systematic method with concern for their safety and mental well-being at the forefront. In some fashion or another, the information was controlled, buffered and then delivered.

Let's jump forward now. The date is April 15th, 2013. The sky was filled with patches of thick, layered clouds with an easy breeze wafting its way through the cordoned off streets of downtown Boston. Men and women of pristine physical condition struggle to maintain the rhythmic synchrony between their breathing and strides. The temperature on this day was a cool 48 degrees when the initial blast of the starting gun echoed through the air for the commencement of the 117th running of the Boston Marathon. That temperature had reached the mid-fifties by the time the first runners had turned the final corner and could now see the finish line, beckoning them like a seductive woman, calling them to cross her and relieve all their pain. By 2:50pm, a number of runners had already experienced the endorphin release associated with the cheering crowd and the slowing of the breathing and shortening of the strides following culmination of the grueling 26 miles. Little did they know how crucial their completion time would actually be.

The two explosions that killed 3 people and injured hundreds more occurred just seconds apart from each other; 12 seconds to be exact. Equally as quick was the spread of information to our children on their social media accounts.

Within a minute, Twitter action with a hashtag referencing the bombing was at 491 tweets. Ten minutes later, almost five thousand tweets. Within just 30 minutes, almost 50,000 tweets, and within less than an hour there were over 100,000 tweets that had been shared (retweeted) over 60,000 times. While this was all happening on Twitter, the Boston Globe released their first tweet 9 minutes after the first explosions and 8 minutes after the first social media posts were believed to have been sent. According to a Twitter analytics company, known as Topsy, they reported that by 4:30 pm that day, over 700,000 mentions of the Boston Marathon occurred on Twitter. That is, over 700,000 people talking about this event in less than 2 hours-time on Twitter.

It was not just written posts and tweets that were shared on social media. Images of injured people, smoke by the finish line and even a Vine video were shared. The Vine video shared by one Twitter user was retweeted over 3,172 times and included the hashtag, #BostonMarathon. In an article published by National Geographic in 2013, Bill Braniff, the Executive Director of the National Consortium for the Study of Terrorism and Response to Terrorism when speaking about the social media reaction to the bombing was quoted as saying: "Authorities have recognized that one of the first places people go in events like this is to social media, to see what the crowd is saying about what to do next, Today authorities went to Twitter and directed them to traditional media environments where authorities could present a clear calm picture of what to do next."

This position clearly came out of a reactionary approach to the spectators, bystanders, and 3rd party misinformed tweeters who were filling the airwaves with partial and incorrect information. It was a dangerous trend during times of crisis; and even more dangerous when coupled with the fear response of children and young adults who are now receiving this information through their social media feeds.

A Story About My Stepdaughter

How bad were the misinformed tweets that day? Well that's an excellent question and one I am so happy you asked. In a story of twisted fate, a young girl who survived the Sandy Hook School shooting, was running in honor of her fallen classmates. Now reread those words and feel your stomach creep up into your throat, imagining the feeling that family was experiencing following all they had been through! That tweet (which actually displayed the young girl running) was false.

As first responders and bystanders raced to come to the rescue of the injured, many others raced to their Twitter accounts to demand that the City of Boston reactivate cell phone service. As we are now aware, cell service was never shut down by the government. The bombs, the bombs were everywhere, at least according to twitter users. Users claimed reports of bombs at Harvard, in Cambridge, in the JFK Library, and other locations, further exacerbating the already widespread panic and fear.

In the end, accurately measuring the result of such misinformation is difficult. However, what is not difficult is identifying there is most surely an effect. A well-known psychological truth is that reshaping an initial belief by a child is far more difficult than forming that belief was in the first place. Media coverage of a traumatic event can undoubtedly lead to increased fears and anxieties in children. Before we can begin to understand these effects, we must first discuss how children process information differently than adults, and then take a look at what type of impact exposure has on children.

Let's begin with an excerpt extracted from an article printed in the National Association of School Psychologists' Communique (March/April 2014. Volume 42, Number 6): "studies that followed children after the tragic events in New York City on September 11, 2001 and the 1995 Oklahoma City bombing found that even children who did not have direct exposure to the attacks could develop symptoms of post-traumatic stress disorder as a result of their exposure to media related to the attacks (Pfefferbaum et al., 2003; Saylor, Cowart, Lipovsky, Jackson, & Finch, 2003)."

When it comes to media coverage of traumatic events, such as school shootings and acts of terrorism, the impact of excessive exposure to media coverage is clearly explained in a recent article by National Association of School Psychologist (2012). As the research indicates, children process trauma differently than their adult counterparts and may face significant challenges understanding their own "emotional and psychological reactions" to such events. Young children are unable to distinguish between their own reality and that which may be depicted on television or online. It isn't until roughly 12 years of age that a child's brain is able to become less egocentric and increase awareness of external events. This does not mean that the child can fully understand the nature and context of traumatic external events occurring and being broadcast on television and social media. In fact, it isn't until around 11 years of age that a child develops a more realistic concept of death and its irreversible nature.

Several studies have looked into both the attacks on September 11th and the Oklahoma City bombings, and their findings indicate that even children who were not directly exposed to the events reported symptoms of PTSD. Furthermore, symptomatology was reported to be more significant in those who had media exposure to these events.

The impact of media exposure of traumatic events on children's functioning can look similar to symptoms of trauma. Children who experience trauma may show early lags in receptive and expressive language, difficulty with sustained attention and concentration, show weaknesses in executive functioning including problem solving, organizing, and planning, and also present with an inability to experience, identify, express, and modulate their emotions. Trauma can also reframe a child's belief about the world around them. For instance, a child who has either experienced a trauma or been exposed to traumatic environments, may develop an "I'm not safe" concept of the world, "People can't be trusted" or "The world is a dangerous place".

When working with children who have been victims of trauma or exposed to traumatic events, it is most important to provide a safe, stable, and understanding environment for the child. Promoting a sense of safety for children can be done by doing the following.

- Set limits around television and social media viewing, because too much exposure can increase fears.
- Provide a consistent structure and routine for children, as this helps to generate a sense of psychological safety.
- Provide a safe place for your children to talk about their fears.
- Encourage healthy and safe coping strategies.
- Use professional help. We don't have to be everything to our children, we simply must acknowledge when they need more than we can give.

In many cases of social media exposure, the recognition of the impact is dismissed, so the above actions are not considered. End result, as fathers, is that our role in shaping our children is far more challenging than ever before, and social media is an untiring foe. A foe that we must get into the ring with, exchange blows, and most importantly, knock the fuck out. Time to man up.

Paint By Numbers

This book was titled *Paint By Numbers* to portray all of our desires to take an art form and provide some clarity to the execution of it. The witticism lies in the conspicuous reality that fatherhood is the most singular expression of all art forms; incapable of draconian structure in its execution. Go out, implement your tailored operations, and create masterpieces for the world to behold. Your tools and instruments will at times need to be heavy and sharp, carving deep impacts on the medium in which you are working. In alternative settings, your implement and tenderness will graze the subject with such hushed sensitivity that impact can only be regarded through attentive perusal.

In one and the other the consequential significance cannot be foreordained. As a result, our only locus of control embeds itself in the daily brush strokes we paint, with persistence and a smatter of luck, the colors and lines will depict our desired impression. In the end, when gazing at our own Mona Lisa's, and listening to the notes of our original versions of American Pie, the subtle variations and idiosyncrasies of our artwork will fill us with delight. An overwhelming feeling of joy in realizing how fucking happy we are that these works of art were never paint by numbers.

Made in the USA
Middletown, DE
30 October 2022